RSb10

Camped this 25th of August

Camped the 24th August

White Stone Creek

This place called by the Indians Hill of Little Devils

Rugged burning bluffs Cobalt &c &c &c

Beautiful Plain

Camped the 23d of August 1804

Blue Bluffs

Beautiful Plain

Camped the 22d of August 1804

Alum Stone Bluffs

Petite Creek

deep

Sioux River

Cobalt, Pyrites, Copperas, & Alum Bluffs

Camped the 21st of August 1804

An ancient Village of the Mahars

Sious or Sioux River

Camped the ... of August 1804

...id Bluffs

...oo Creek

Camped 19th 14th 15th 16th and 17th of August 1804 Latitude 42° 13'41' N.

Sergeant C. Floyd 20th of August 1804 was buried this

Floyds River

Trading House

The American Exploration and Travel Series

George Catlin, *Floyd's Grave, Where Lewis and Clark Buried Sergeant Floyd in 1804*, 1832.
Oil on canvas, 11¼ × 14⅜ in. Smithsonian American Art Museum, Gift of Mrs. Joseph Harrison Jr.

Exploring with Lewis and Clark

The 1804 Journal of Charles Floyd

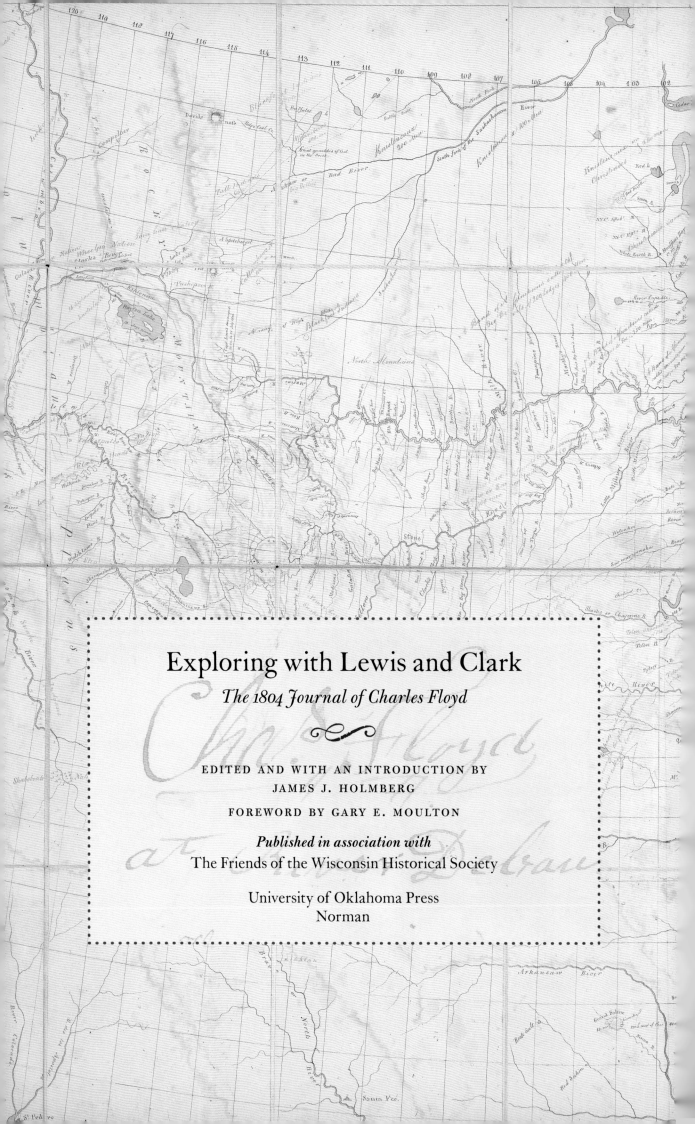

Exploring with Lewis and Clark

The 1804 Journal of Charles Floyd

EDITED AND WITH AN INTRODUCTION BY
JAMES J. HOLMBERG

FOREWORD BY GARY E. MOULTON

Published in association with
The Friends of the Wisconsin Historical Society

University of Oklahoma Press
Norman

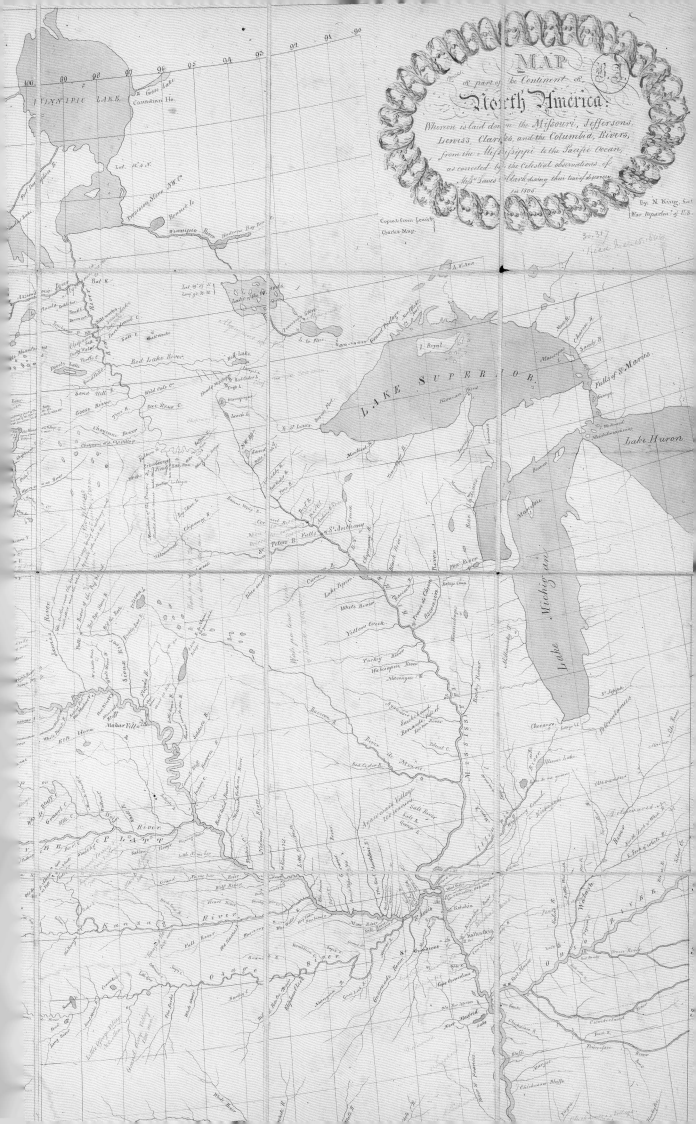

MAP
of part of the Continent of
North America:
Whereon is laid down the Missouri, Jeffersons,
Lewis's, Clarkes, and the Columbia, Rivers,
from the Mississippi to the Pacific Ocean,
as corrected by the Celestial observations of
Messrs Lewis & Clark during their tour of discovery
in 1806.

By. N. King. Sculp.
War Departmt of U.S.

Copied from Lewis &
Clarks Map.

LAKE SUPERIOR

Lake Huron

Michigan Lake

WINNIPIC LAKE.

PLATTE

KANZAS River

OSAGE

Exploring with Lewis and Clark: The 1804 Journal of Charles Floyd is Volume 80 in The American Exploration and Travel Series.

∞ The paper in this book meets the guidelines for permanence and durability of the Committee on Production Guidelines for Book Longevity of the Council on Library Resources, Inc.

1 2 3 4 5 6 7 8 9 10

Library of Congress Cataloging-in-Publication Data
Floyd, Charles, d. 1804.
    Exploring with Lewis and Clark: the 1804 journal of Charles Floyd / edited and with an introduction by James J. Holmberg ; foreword by Gary E. Moulton.
      p. cm. — (The American exploration and travel series ; v. 80)
    Includes bibliographical references and index.
    ISBN 0-8061-3674-x (alk. paper)
    1. Floyd, Charles, d. 1804—Diaries. 2. Explorers—West (U.S.)—Diaries. 3. Lewis and Clark Expedition (1804–1806). 4. West (U.S.)—Discovery and exploration. 5. Frontier and pioneer life—West (U.S.). 6. West (U.S.)—Description and travel. 7. Overland journeys to the Pacific. I. Holmberg, James J. (James John), 1958-. II. Title. III. Series.
    F592.5.F58 2005
    917.804'2—dc22   2004055384

Front endsheets: Clark-Maximilian map showing the location of Charles Floyd's grave and a stretch of the Missouri River. This copy was made in 1833 from original expedition maps in William Clark's possession. Credit: Joslyn Art Museum

Back endsheets: Route of the Lewis and Clark Expedition across the continent. Credit: National Park Service

Pages iv–v: Lewis and Clark's Map of 1806 showing the segment of the trail traveled by Charles Floyd—from the Falls of the Ohio (at the edge of the map above Silver Creek) in the east to Floyds River and the site of his death in the west. Credit: Boston Athenaeum

Copyedited by Amy Smith Bell
Proofread by Carrie Wicks
Designed and typeset by Susan E. Kelly, Luminant Studio
Produced by Marquand Books, Inc., Seattle
   www.marquand.com
Color separations by iocolor, Seattle
Printed and bound by CS Graphics Pte., Ltd., Singapore

Foreword

WE KNOW TOO LITTLE OF SERGEANT CHARLES FLOYD, THE ONLY
member of Meriwether Lewis and William Clark's Corps of Discovery to die on
that famous exploration. Lewis's assessment of the sergeant, "a young man of much
merit," gives only a hint of the man and his contributions to the Corps. As with
so much else about the expedition, we want more. But Floyd's journal hardly provides the stuff for a biography or the material to make an epic of the expedition. Yet
despite the limited scope of the sergeant's journal (fifty-six pages covering the first
three months of the journey) and the brevity of his entries (mostly running no more
than a few lines), I find instances in Floyd's journal that give insight into the Corps
not seen in the other journalists' accounts. On 7 August 1804, for example, Floyd is
the only writer to say that Moses Reed deserted the party, "with out aney Jest Case."
In Floyd's mind the Corps must already have become that "band of brothers" so
often alluded to in fiction but so infrequently formed in fact. Floyd must have believed
that Reed deserted his comrades-in-arms without the usual causes given for such
action. The soldier had not been under the strain of combat, had not faced the harsh
whip of stern commanders, nor had he apparently fallen into difficulties with his fellow soldiers. Whatever caused Reed to desert, to Floyd it was not justified. Through
his journal entries, Floyd shows us the loyal soldier, committed to the cause, and
does not understand those who could not see the importance of the mission or the
brotherhood being shaped in the common struggle to succeed.

Enter James J. Holmberg with a new edition of the sergeant's short journal. In
contrast to my own editing of Floyd's journal, with its restricted annotation due to
the detailed notes of earlier volumes, Jim provides full treatment to the sergeant's
entries. He also furnishes something quite rare in editing circles: facsimiles of every
page in the original journal. Such pairing allows users to compare the editor's transcription with their own reading of Floyd's writing. I salute Jim's valor and give him
fair warning: in the few instances where the writings of Lewis and Clark were dis-
played in my edition (those connected with illustrations from their journals), careful
readers found discrepancies and sent me alternate transcriptions. Jim already admits
to differences with my own transcriptions. He'll doubtless hear about counter ren-
derings of his text—but not from me. I applaud his efforts and find here the very
result I'd hoped for, a splendid example of new scholarship on the expedition.

Jim has already distinguished himself as a gifted editor with the publication of
his book *Dear Brother: Letters of William Clark to Jonathan Clark* (2002). Here he
continues that tradition and again demonstrates curiosity, comprehensiveness, and
depth of research. If any new journals from the expedition are discovered in the years
to come, I'm going to let Jim do the editing.

Gary E. Moulton
Lincoln, Nebraska

I am going away. I want you to write me a letter.

Charles Floyd, 20 August 1804

*We buried him at the top of the bluff . . . with the Honors of War
much lamented; . . . This Man at all times gave us proofs of his firmness
and Deturmined resolution to doe Service to his Countrey
and honor to himself.*

William Clark regarding Charles Floyd, 20 August 1804

Preface

AS A NATIVE OF LOUISVILLE, KENTUCKY, I GREW UP HEARING THE name Floyd. In a historical context, it primarily meant Colonel John Floyd, one of the state's early leaders. A Louisville apartment complex now occupies the site of his pioneer station. I lived in that complex for two years and enjoyed visiting the station's surviving springhouse and family cemetery and musing on the lives of these pioneers. I did not know it at the time, but it is believed that Charles Floyd was born at this, his uncle's settlement and he definitely grew up in the area. I unknowingly had roamed over the same ground that Charles had growing up.

When I began working at The Filson Historical Society, I enjoyed perusing its vast collections. Curiosity and a desire to learn about Kentucky's and our nation's heritage led to many rewarding experiences. One such experience was coming across a file of old photographs that froze a series of historical events in time. Those events were the two reburials of Sergeant Charles Floyd and the building of the Floyd Monument in Sioux City, Iowa. These scenes on the banks of the Missouri River as captured in 1895, 1900, and 1901 fascinated me. Here was a Kentuckian, a Louisvillian, who had gone west with Lewis and Clark, never to return. Here was the only member of the expedition to die on the journey whose ironic fate it was to have a monument rise above his grave that was larger than anything dedicated to the members of the Corps of Discovery who *did* reach the Pacific.

I consequently sought out additional information on Floyd and found very little. He died early on the expedition and little was known about his life before the journey. In 1996, when the Lewis and Clark Trail Heritage Foundation held its annual meeting in Sioux City, I proposed writing an article about Floyd's grave and monument in the Foundation's magazine, *We Proceeded On*. What was intended as a rather brief essay showcasing photos of the Floyd Monument evolved into a lengthy and detailed account of the sergeant's grave and memorial. Actually editing the journal of Charles Floyd never occurred to me during my growing education about this heroic young explorer.

It is often true that from little things come big things. Roaming across the area of Charles Floyd's birthplace was a little thing, of no seeming consequence. Looking at the photographs of his grave and monument seemed a little thing. But from them came the impetus for my 1996 article. Writing that article, together with the experience of editing *Dear Brother,* in turn has led to *Exploring with Lewis and Clark: The 1804 Journal of Charles Floyd.* Floyd's life and monument are worthy of notice. His journal is worth reading. Viewing every page of his expedition account is a rare opportunity indeed. I hope the reader will find the story of this "young man of much merit" and his monument as fascinating as I have.

Acknowledgments

THIS FACSIMILE EDITION OF THE JOURNAL OF CHARLES FLOYD would not have been possible without the assistance and commitment of a number of institutions, groups, and individuals. You meet many special people in the course of working on a project, and this one was no exception. Thank you to the Wisconsin Historical Society for permission to publish this facsimile and print edition of the Floyd journal. Despite a tight schedule, this project came together benefitting from the usual editorial and publishing standards due to the cooperation and efforts of the University of Oklahoma Press and its editor Charles E. Rankin. Thank you to Chuck and the staff of OU Press, as well as to editor Amy Smith Bell, designer Susan E. Kelly, proofreader Carrie Wicks, and Ed Marquand and the staff of Marquand Books. Their efforts and talents in producing this book are very much appreciated.

Every project has a driving force. This project's catalysts were the Friends of the Wisconsin Historical Society and Friends member Charles "Chuck" Hatfield. Led by Chuck, the Friends were determined to make this volume a reality and provided funding, work, and encouragement to accomplish it. Chuck essentially served as project director. He raised funds and did other important work to help make this edition of Floyd's journal a reality. My thanks also go to Dee Ducklow, president of the Friends, and the Friends board of trustees for their support.

A number of donors contributed financially to the project in addition to the Friends of the Wisconsin Historical Society itself. Appreciation is extended to the U.S. Army Corps of Engineers; and the Badger State Chapter of the Lewis and Clark Trail Heritage Foundation, especially members Jim Rosenberger, Dave Bubier, Todd Berens, and Thomas and Mary Butts. Thanks to Richard Larson of the Friends, who made the first donation in support of the project. The support of the Kohler Foundation, Lewis and Clark Trail Heritage Foundation, Clark-Floyd Counties Convention and Tourism Bureau, Bill and Janet Smith, Mac and Tori Murden McClure, and the Falls of the Ohio Lewis and Clark Bicentennial Committee is also appreciated.

My thanks to Harry Miller and Carolyn Mattern of the Wisconsin Historical Society and Matt Blessing of Marquette University for their assistance and expertise concerning my questions about the Floyd journal and the Draper Manuscripts. Rebecca Rice of The Filson Historical Society, Larry Mensching of the Joslyn Art Museum, Sally Pierce and Patricia Boulos of the Boston Athenaeum, Richard Sorenson of the Smithsonian Institution, and Richard Williams of the Lewis and Clark National Historic Trail, National Park Service, were all very cooperative regarding the acquisition of illustrations and maps. Bob Clark, of the Arthur H. Clark Company, provided welcome counsel in the early stages of the project. Speculation about the cause of Floyd's death led to interesting discussions. Chuck Hatfield,

Jim Rosenberger, and Ted Steinbock provided additional information and interesting thoughts about Floyd's illness. Gwen Hatfield deserves special thanks for her patience and understanding during the many hours her husband devoted to this project.

I also want to thank the late V. Strode Hinds and his wife, Beverly, of Sioux City. Strode provided important research material for my 1996 monument article in *We Proceeded On;* I used that research again for this project. He was an untiring supporter of the monument and the Lewis and Clark legacy. Bev Hinds continues those efforts today and also sent me some additional material.

This edition of the Floyd journal is fortunate to have a Foreword by Gary E. Moulton, the perfect person to have written it. His masterful editing of *The Journals of the Lewis and Clark Expedition* is the definitive edition and serves as a model for other projects. It was a crucial resource for me in this project.

Finally, I thank my family for their support during this project. My wife, Ruthe, and my children, Elise, Aaron, and Emily, are good soldiers in their own right and are unfailingly encouraging and uncomplaining.

Editorial Note

In preparing this edition of the Floyd journal, I have generally followed accepted, current editorial practices. That is to say: edit the document as lightly as possible, leaving it in its original form—including errors and all—while making only changes necessary for clarity and understanding. Brackets enclose material that has been added to the original or was written by someone other than Floyd. In the case of the latter, the person is identified. I have followed some unorthodox practices, namely: using the strikethrough feature to indicate words that have been crossed out, the superscript feature to illustrate abbreviated words, and a caret-type feature to note insertions in the journal, either by Floyd or someone else. The theory in doing this, rather than using other editorial symbols to indicate these textual features, is that it best reflects the original text.

Floyd sometimes used an "x" and perhaps a caret "‸" to insert material. Others used the latter symbol as necessary. The words or letters appearing between these symbols (alone in their first use and bracketed in their subsequent use to indicate the end of the inserted material) generally appear above the line of text in which they are intended to be inserted. Brackets enclosing the initial caret indicate that Floyd made no actual insertion mark. The sergeant also often made additions and insertion marks in the vicinity of where he intended the insertion to be—sometimes in the correct place, sometimes after the sentence they should have preceded, and sometimes under the sentence itself indicating the insertion relates to that sentence and should be placed either before or after it accordingly. His meaning is indicated as accurately as possible. Brackets are also used to insert a letter or word that is missing or misspelled in order to clarify Floyd's meaning. This is done as seldom as possible. Floyd used inkblots, ink smears, strikethroughs, and overwrites to indicate deletions and revisions. The strikethrough feature is used here to denote this Floyd editorial practice. Because he used almost no punctuation, an extra space has been inserted between sentences to better clarify sentences and text for the reader.

In this edition the reader has the benefit of seeing illustrations of every page of Floyd's journal. Having a transcript of an original document together with images of the original is a special opportunity for the reader to enjoy something of a virtual experience in seeing and reading the original, while at the same time being able to take advantage of the printed and annotated copy. The transcription is as literal as possible. Editing an original document is a subjective business, especially in producing the transcript. That is even more true when the author's handwriting and grammar are a challenge. William Clark has a well-deserved reputation for his creative spelling. But in truth, Clark was an educated and literate man with good penmanship whose spelling abilities far exceeded those of many other members of the expedition and the general population of the early nineteenth century.

Charles Floyd is a clear case in point. His grammar and spelling leave much to be desired compared with that of his captains. Yet he got the information down on paper and left a three-month record of his experience with the Corps. I have provided as accurate a transcription as possible. But knowing what Floyd wrote—or intended to write—was a challenge at times. Erratic spelling compounds general poor spelling. To this add handwriting that does not always form the letters you think must be intended—unless of course he wrote the word the way he pronounced it. Phonetic spelling was common two hundred years ago, and spellers then did not have the benefit of a dictionary. This consequently required me to make many decisions—if not educated guesses—as to what certain letters and sometimes words the author intended. In some cases I have made a subjective decision. That "a" might be an "o" or that "e" might be an undotted "i" as actually intended by Floyd and in someone else's opinion. When readers can read the transcript and compare it to the original—page by page in this book—they can decide for themselves about such things. And it is a foregone conclusion that not everyone will agree with me. In a rare instance (one hopes) it might be an editorial error. More likely, however, it will be a difference of opinion as to what young Sergeant Floyd wrote.

Many readers will undoubtedly be familiar with and will have read Gary E. Moulton's masterful edition of *The Journals of the Lewis and Clark Expedition*. A comparison of his transcript of the Floyd journal with this one will reveal a number of differences. In most cases the differences are due to editorial practices and decisions regarding certain letters and words. This in no way diminishes the value and importance of Moulton's edition—or this one for that matter. They vary in small ways transcriptually, subjectively, and editorially.

The reader will enjoy fuller annotation in this volume than in previous editions of the Floyd journal. This is due primarily to its publication as a separate volume. The best known and most widely used editions of Floyd's journal are volume nine in Moulton's *Journals* series, published in 1995, in which it was paired with Sergeant John Ordway's journal and the Reuben Gold Thwaites 1904–5 edition of *The Original Journals of the Lewis and Clark Expedition, 1804–1806* that included the then recently discovered Floyd journal as volume seven. The latter had essentially no annotation for Floyd's journal. The annotation for the Moulton edition is light and comments essentially on matters not mentioned in or that are contradictory to William Clark's journal. This is understandable. Those wanting more information are directed to consult the notes for the Clark journal in volume three. The Moulton edition is this edition's primary source of information for the notes, especially for the identification of people and places Floyd mentions. In striking a balance regarding the notes, not everyone or everything is identified. Those wanting to know the present-day names of the creeks and rivers mentioned or the hunters sent out should consult Moulton and other sources. I have only identified such when deemed appropriate relative to the nature of the entry. Other questions of a possible editorial or informational nature are usually dealt with in the notes.

It is a rather unique and most welcome opportunity to publish a facsimile edition of the Floyd journal. I hope that the readers will enjoy and find useful this journal of exploration left to posterity by Charles Floyd.

Exploring with Lewis and Clark

The 1804 Journal of Charles Floyd

The southeastern section of Lewis and Clark's Map of 1806 showing the segment of the trail traveled by Charles Floyd—from the Falls of the Ohio (at the edge of the map above Silver Creek) in the east to Floyd's River and the site of his death in the west.
Credit: Boston Athenaeum

Introduction

The Life, Death, and Monument of Charles Floyd
"a young man of much merit"

James J. Holmberg

The Lewis and Clark Expedition is known as the greatest exploring venture in the history of the United States. Over the course of three years, a group of explorers known as the Corps of Discovery traveled across the American West to the Pacific and then back again. Made up of soldiers, civilians, a woman, a slave, and a dog, the Corps accomplished their mission because of talent, leadership, courage, cooperation, and luck. They came together not only as a disciplined and focused military unit but also as a family, dedicated to and supportive of each other. If Captains Meriwether Lewis and William Clark had miscalculated and misstepped early in the expedition, it is possible that events might have turned out differently, and the Lewis and Clark Expedition would then be a little remembered historical footnote. But the captains chose well, trained well, and led well, and thus they and their expedition are admired and studied two hundred years after their western journey.

An important part of this successful expedition began at the Falls of the Ohio River in the summer of 1803. Co-captain William Clark had moved across the river from Louisville to Clarksville, Indiana Territory, that spring to start over. In trying to help his famous brother, General George Rogers Clark, with his tangled legal and financial affairs, William Clark had impoverished himself. His friend Meriwether Lewis's letter arrived at a perfect moment in Clark's life. The adventure of the journey as well as its possible rewards appealed to him. Clark knew that they would be performing an important mission for the United States, and if they succeeded the rewards that undoubtedly would follow in the form of land grants and possible government appointments might assure his future success. He immediately agreed to join the undertaking and to recruit young hunters and woodsmen for it.[1]

The Falls area was the perfect place to do so. Louisville was the last major town on the Ohio River, a major transportation route westward. It was from there that frontiersmen and pioneers often departed on their western adventures. The rugged and talented hunters from the Falls region were needed to help feed the Corps. They were the young men who had either been born in Kentucky or moved there as children. They had grown up on the frontier, learning all the skills necessary to survive on the frontier and the wilderness. These were the "good hunters, stout, healthy, unmarried men, accustomed to the woods, and capable of bearing bodily fatigue in a pretty considerable degree" that Lewis asked Clark to recruit.[2] They would become

The completed Floyd Monument looking across the Missouri River from Nebraska, ca. 1901.
Credit: The Filson Historical Society

members of the famous "Nine Young Men from Kentucky," part of the nucleus—that all-important foundation—of the Corps of Discovery formed at the Falls of the Ohio in October 1803.

William Clark already knew some of the young men who would be valuable members of the expedition and he wasted no time recruiting them. On 24 July 1803 he wrote Lewis that he had "temperally engaged some men for the enterprise" whom he believed were capable of the expedition's demands. Almost a month later, on 21 August, Clark reported that he had promised to engage four young men on the expedition who were the "best woodsmen & Hunters, of young men in this part of the Countrey."[3] Although official acceptance perhaps had to wait until Lewis arrived in Louisville on 14 October, three of the men were such sure things and so committed to the endeavor that they bear enlistment dates of 1 August, two and a half months before Lewis and Clark actually joined forces. They were the first three permanent enlisted members of the Corps of Discovery. They were Charles Floyd and brothers Joseph and Reubin Field.[4] The Field brothers served through the entire expedition and received high praise from Lewis in his post-expedition report. Floyd had made a good impression also, and Lewis's assessment might have been even more flattering for this "young man of much merit" except for one tragic fact—Floyd died near present Sioux City, Iowa, on 20 August 1804, the only fatality in the Corps of Discovery.[5]

Who was this young explorer and soldier who had gained the confidence and trust of Lewis and Clark and demonstrated such potential? Little is known of Charles Floyd's life before the expedition. He was a member of one of Kentucky's prominent pioneer families. His uncle, John Floyd, penetrated Kentucky in the mid-1770s as a surveyor working for his mentor, William Preston of Virginia. Kentucky at that time was part of Virginia's huge frontier Fincastle County. In 1776, Kentucky County was created, and in 1780 it was divided into the counties of Fayette, Jefferson, and Lincoln. Floyd cast his lot with Kentucky and became one of its early leaders. He also had secured title to large tracts of land, and in 1779 he settled on one of these in Jefferson County near the frontier village of Louisville.[6]

John Floyd did not come to Kentucky alone. As did thousands of other pioneers, the Floyds moved to Kentucky as a family. In the fall of 1779 they left Amherst County, Virginia, and traveled by way of the Cumberland Gap and the Wilderness Road to Floyd's Station on the Middle Fork of Beargrass Creek. With this group were John Floyd's brother Robert Clark Floyd and his family. Robert had married Lilleyan Hampton some time before 1773. They had two children when they moved to Kentucky, and two more were born afterward. The Floyds farmed and with other settlers sought to wrest Kentucky from the Indians. Robert Floyd served in the militia under George Rogers Clark, including duty as a scout, and eventually rose to the rank of major. A brutal twenty-year war was waged along the frontier. Indian attacks were an ever-present threat, and Kentuckians launched their own campaigns of death and destruction against Indian towns north of the Ohio River. It was into this frontier environment that Charles Floyd was born about 1782. Other additions were also being made to the extended Floyd family, but there were losses as well. In April 1783, John Floyd was killed by Indians.[7]

Charles Floyd grew up in this frontier Kentucky. Self-reliance, vigilance, resourcefulness, a sense of duty, and other traits all combined with frontier skills to help assure survival. Even then, life could come to an abrupt end through violence or disease. Although Charles would not have remembered his uncle John, he undoubtedly heard stories about his adventures, as well as about that of his own father's and other pioneers. The threat of Indian attack was ever present until 1794, when Charles was about twelve years old. In August of that year Anthony Wayne's army defeated the confederation of Northwestern tribes at Fallen Timbers. Young Charles would have worked on his father's farm and performed a variety of other chores. He received some schooling, enough to be literate, as evidenced by his expedition journal. His handwriting was deliberate and his spelling poor, but he could read and write.

Perhaps seeking a better opportunity, Robert Floyd moved across the Ohio to Clarksville Township by 1799. In 1803, Floyd and his oldest son, Davis, operated a ferry at the foot of the Falls, from Clarksville to the Kentucky shore, where the road from the foot of the Falls led to Louisville. Charles might have helped with the boat, gaining some experience for his future exploring endeavor. The abilities that enabled him to be a prized expedition recruit and sergeant were in evidence by 1802. By that year, some twenty-year-old Charles was named the constable of Clarksville Township. Keeping the peace and performing various judicial duties was a very responsible position for someone so young. In July 1802 he was awarded the contract to carry the mail between Louisville and Vincennes. This was a weekly 220-mile round-trip through country that was still largely unsettled. Charles would have traveled the route on horseback, his supplies and mailbags slung to each side, or perhaps with a packhorse in tow. Always on the lookout for potential trouble, he would have made his own camp at night or stayed at an available house or tavern. Whether Charles's brother-in-law, Louisville postmaster Thomas M. Winn, arranged for his relative to receive this lucrative contract is not known; but given what is known about Floyd, one can assume that he successfully carried the mail over this daunting route.[8]

In the spring of 1803, William Clark and George Rogers Clark settled at Point of Rocks on the eastern edge of Clarksville. Their farm was at the foot of the Falls of the Ohio and had a commanding and beautiful view of them. Two miles upriver at the head of the Falls, Louisville could be seen. The Clarks almost certainly used the Floyds's ferry to go back and forth across the river. It is also possible that Charles sometimes delivered their mail from the Louisville post office to Clarksville. Perhaps one of those letters was Meriwether Lewis's invitation to William Clark to join him on the expedition to the Pacific and recruit young men for the enterprise.

What Charles did over the summer and early fall of 1803 while awaiting Lewis's arrival is not known. He likely continued his work as post rider and constable and might have assisted Clark regarding expedition recruitment. How involved his affairs were is unknown, but he most likely spent some time putting his affairs in order in anticipation of the Corps' departure westward. He probably visited family and friends. His uncle, Charles Floyd, and cousins lived along Mill Creek in southwestern Jefferson County. This was the neighborhood from which the Field brothers hailed. They had grown up on nearby Pond Creek, and the area was collectively known as the Pond Creek Settlement. Floyd apparently was close to his cousins, as evidenced later by their sadness upon receiving news of his death, and he may have known the Field brothers as well.[9]

As summer became fall, a regular watch would have been kept on the Louisville waterfront for Lewis's keelboat. When it finally came into site on 14 October and landed at Louisville, Clark almost certainly was there to meet his partner in discovery. It is possible that Floyd was at his side. Over the next two weeks, the keelboat and red pirogue were piloted through the Falls, six more recruits were enlisted, affairs were put in order, good-byes were said, and final arrangements were made. On 26 October the boats, bearing the nucleus of the Corps of Discovery, pushed off from Clarksville down the Ohio and into history. They would not return for three years. Charles Floyd would never return.

Progress down the Ohio to its confluence with the Mississippi was steady but slow. The river was higher than the low water that had plagued Lewis in descending the river from Pittsburgh, but it was still low enough to impede an easy float downstream. With scattered farms and hamlets on the Kentucky bank and wilderness on the Indiana bank, the explorers proceeded to Fort Massac, where the next group of recruits, including George Drouillard, joined them. Five days of observation and reconnoitering were done at the confluence. Then the upstream trip to Kaskaskia, Cahokia, and St. Louis was made. Recruits from the U.S. post at Kaskaskia provided most of the rest of the Corps. By mid-December, Lewis and Clark had verified that the Spanish would not allow them to proceed up the Missouri until the Louisiana Territory was officially turned over to the United States (which occurred on 10 March 1804). Consequently, the party sailed northward to a place opposite the mouth of the Missouri, where they established Camp Dubois near the confluence of the Mississippi and Wood (or Dubois) Rivers. This was the first of what ultimately would be three winter camps during the expedition.[10]

Life for the explorers-in-waiting settled into a pattern that winter of 1803–4. Lewis spent much of the winter in Cahokia and St. Louis gathering information and conducting business. Clark spent most of his time at the Wood River camp, preparing the men and the boats for a spring departure. Existing evidence indicates that Floyd was an important aide during this time. Clark had him carry the first dispatches from Camp Dubois to Lewis and the post office in Cahokia, about twenty miles away. He performed courier duty throughout the winter and into the spring. Lewis expressed similar confidence in Floyd. On 20 February 1804, Lewis issued detachment orders regarding command of the camp during the absence of both Clark and himself in St. Louis. Sergeant John Ordway was placed in overall command but Floyd was also given an important responsibility. Lewis ordered that "Floyd will take charge of our quartes and store and be exempt from guard duty untill our return, the commanding Officer hopes that this proof of his confidence will be justifyed by the rigid performance of the orders given him on that subject." He addressed the orders to Floyd, so Charles apparently was in charge of seeing that they were read and posted. He was again assigned this duty on 7 April, when both captains were in St. Louis: "Sergt. Floyd will stay in our quarters, attend to them, and the Store; and to the other duties required of him; he will also assist Sergt. Ordway as much as possable."[11] But Floyd did get to roam the woods and prairies hunting on occasion. Not long after arriving at Wood River, Clark sent Floyd and fellow Kentuckian John Shields out hunting and they brought in "7 Turkeys verry fat."[12]

Adjusting to military life was not easy for some of the Kentuckians. Reubin Field and Shields were both taken to task by Lewis in detachment orders dated 3 March. Floyd apparently experienced no such problems. In those same orders, Lewis directed that the entire party was to follow Ordway's orders as directed by the captains with the exception of Floyd, who had been "specially directed to perform other duties." Lewis and Clark clearly believed that Floyd could perform the duties of a sergeant. But another reason also might have been factored into their evaluation. Floyd was probably closer than any other member of the Corps to being from the same level of society as Lewis and Clark. The Floyd family consisted of landowners, business owners, men involved in civic affairs, officers in the militia, and longtime Clark family friends. The captains and Floyd had much in common. Beyond this, Lewis and Clark had confidence and trust in him to perform the duties of a non-commissioned officer. This was confirmed on 1 April, when Floyd, Ordway, as well as Floyd's first cousin and fellow Kentuckian Nathaniel H. Pryor were appointed sergeants. Each was placed in command of a squad. Floyd commanded the Second Squad. Demonstrating that connection between them, Floyd's squad included Joseph and Reubin Field.[13]

By mid-May the waiting was over. Upper Louisiana was now officially a part of the United States, the winter ice and floods were gone, and final preparations were complete. On 14 May 1804 the Corps of Discovery started up the Missouri River. Two days later they reached St. Charles and delayed there until Lewis joined them after concluding business in St. Louis. He arrived on 20 May and the next day they "proceeded on under a jentle Breese."[14] The journey of exploration into the American West itself had now begun.

Floyd kept a journal of the day-to-day progress of the expedition. Others, including Clark, Ordway, Patrick Gass, and Joseph Whitehouse also kept journals during the ascent of the lower Missouri. They would continue their journals to journey's end. Floyd's would end three months later, when his own journey was abruptly ended by death. But that was three months in the future, and in mid-May he was recording the basic activities and experiences of the Corps of Discovery. Through his and the others' journals we can follow the progress, experiences, and adventures of this young explorer and his companions as they ascended the Missouri.

Working boats upstream against the current and obstructions of the Missouri was hard work. Floyd and the other journalists regularly recorded their struggle to move forward. The two pirogues faced the same challenges as the keelboat but negotiated them with greater ease. The main daily struggle was to move the keelboat upstream. It was the Corps' main craft, and the permanent Corps members—the three squads commanded by the sergeants—were assigned to it. The day-to-day working of the boats, like life in camp, was routine. The men did not consider such details remarkable, and consequently something not worthy of comment. To the historian and reader today, however, a description of such activities would be priceless. Imagine if Floyd or Clark or one of the other journal keepers had written detailed descriptions of the scenes around the campfires; of breaking camp and moving out for another day of discovery; of working the boats upriver. Instead, we see glimpses of this through offhand remarks and observation. We can also gain a better understanding through the periodic detachment orders. One such order was issued on 26 May, as the Corps began to settle into a regular routine and rhythm on the river. It provides an understanding of the operation—and hence life—aboard the keelboat.[15]

The squads of Floyd, Pryor, and Ordway formed the crew of the keelboat. The sergeants rotated daily from the helm, to the center, and then to the bow. Once ashore the men had camp duties. On the days that Floyd was stationed in the helm of the boat he was responsible for steering the boat, attending to the compass when necessary, and seeing that the baggage on the quarterdeck was properly stowed and no loose items obstructed passage between the berths. At night in camp he would oversee his squad pitching their tents, building cooking fires, and preparing meals. He was exempt from actually doing such work, however. Ordway was in charge of issuing provisions to each mess and making arrangements for the next day's guard duty. All the rations would be cooked and a portion reserved for meals while on the following day's march. Floyd would make sure that the men of his squad shared duties equally. The next morning, before getting under way, Floyd paraded the new guard, relieved the sergeant and old guard who had pulled duty that night, and then took up his station in the middle of the boat for that day.

Being in charge of the middle—or center—of the boat entailed a number of responsibilities. Positioning himself on the rear of the starboard locker, Floyd commanded the guard; managed the sails; supervised the men at the oars, the men coming on board, and departure time in the morning; kept a lookout for all watercourses, islands, and other notable features and immediately reported them to the captains; issued spirituous liquors (the beloved whiskey ration!); and regulated rest breaks and stops. Whenever the boat landed, Floyd posted a sentinel on the bank, near the boat, and then he and two other guards reconnoitered the immediate area, going out at least one hundred paces (some 300 feet). When the Corps encamped for the night, he immediately posted two guards, one near the boat and the other a proper distance in the rear of the camp. That night he supervised the guards. When the guard was relieved, he and the guards going off duty made at least a 150 pace (some 450 feet) circuit around the camp and also inspected the keelboat and pirogues to verify their safety.

Morning no doubt came all too soon after these nocturnal duties. Next in the rotation, the young explorer was stationed in the bow of the boat. Constant diligence was demanded in all the positions, but tired or not from the previous night's labors, the sergeant in the bow had to be alert. Floyd had to peer constantly upstream for any dangers that they might be approaching—or that might be approaching them. The detachment orders specifically listed dangers such as an enemy or obstruction in the river. Either could be disastrous to the expedition. Upon seeing any boats, hunting camps, or Indians, Floyd promptly informed the sergeant in the center, who in turn informed the captains. If a snag, sandbar, or other water hazard loomed, he passed word directly to the sergeant at the helm. So there in the bow of the boat Floyd was stationed, with setting pole in hand, ready to assist the bowsman in poling and managing the bow of the boat. He was also the communications officer between the keelboat and the pirogues and any parties on shore, giving and answering all signals established for communication between them and the keelboat.[16]

This three-day rotation of duties provided some variety but little respite from work and diligence. This was a military expedition, with possible danger around every bend of the river. The sergeants bore a tremendous amount of responsibility. They had to have the confidence and support not only of Lewis and Clark but of the men as well. This was a confidence and respect earned by leadership and example. All indications are that Floyd and his fellow sergeants enjoyed that. Just as Floyd had shouldered the responsibilities of constable and wilderness post rider before the expedition, he did the same as a sergeant in the Corps of Discovery.

This was Floyd's life on the Lewis and Clark Expedition. It was a daily grind of exhausting work and responsibility balanced by the wonders of discovery and the beauty of the land. An occasional opportunity to roam on shore or hunt must have been welcomed. At some time during the day, perhaps around their fires at night, he and his fellow sergeants had been ordered to record "all passing occurences, and such other observations on the country &c. as shall appear to them worthy of notice."[17] After a hard day's work this might have been an unwelcome chore. The surviving journals reflect the waxing and waning interest in this duty. It is clear that liberal consultation, comparison, and borrowing occurred between the journal keepers, including Lewis and Clark. Although the entries are often brief, and for the most part contain only the basic events of their busy and exhausting day, the journals indicate that most journal keepers, including Floyd, carried out this charge faithfully.

As the men worked their way up the Missouri that spring and summer, the bonding that had begun among the first recruits at the Falls of the Ohio in 1803 and continued with the larger group during the winter at Camp Dubois continued and became stronger. Although some disciplinary problems occasionally occurred, they became rare. Those who were not dedicated to their comrades and their mission were weeded out. The Corps increasingly became a cohesive, experienced, and dedicated unit determined to accomplish their mission for their country, their president, and for each other. They also became something of a family—even more so after the Charbonneaus joined them in 1805—caring and worrying about one another.

The role Charles Floyd would have played in the entire expedition is unknown. One can expect that he would have continued as a sergeant, further maturing in that position, making an important contribution to the expedition's success and leaving a significant chronicle of his and the Corps' experience. But we will never know. By late July there were hints that all was not well with Sergeant Charles Floyd.

"Serjt. Floyd verry unwell a bad Cold & c," recorded William Clark in his journal entry for Monday, 30 July 1804. Floyd himself, being the good soldier he was and apparently not wanting to complain, did not mention his illness until 31 July, the day after Clark first mentioned it. Even then, he only recorded that he was "verry Sick and Has ben for Somtime but have Recovered my helth again." Sergeant Ordway noted in his journal on that same date that Floyd had been "Sick Several days but now is Gitting Some better."[18] Whether this was the initial phase of the appendicitis and eventual ruptured appendix and peritonitis that is the most widely believed cause of Floyd's death is not known. Medical science of the early nineteenth century did not recognize nor understand such an ailment. A successful appendectomy was years away. Thus it would not have mattered if the malady had struck Floyd in the Philadelphia office of the renowned Dr. Benjamin Rush—much less some 950 miles up the Missouri River. If these first mentions of Floyd's illness were indeed only a "cold," as Clark described it, it must have been a truly terrible one.

The Corps continued upriver unaware that Floyd was not well and an infection apparently was working its poison on him. Three weeks later, on 19 August, the journal keepers recorded that Floyd was again very ill. Some of the entries are almost identical, providing an example of the men copying from each other's journals. Clark recorded that "Serjeant Floyd was taken violently bad with the Beliose Cholick and is dangerously ill we attempt in Vain to releive him, I am much concerned for his Situation — we could get nothing to Stay on his Stomach a moment nature appear exosting fast in him every man is attentive to him ~~york prlly~~ [principally?]."[19]

It is not surprising that everyone was concerned. Floyd apparently was liked by his fellow explorers and highly thought of by the captains. It is also understandable that Clark's slave, York, was particularly attentive to him. They undoubtedly knew each other before the expedition because of the Clark–Floyd family association and the various duties and work each performed that probably brought them into contact. The months spent together since the summer of 1803, when Clark began assembling his expedition recruits, certainly allowed each man to get to know the other. The concern of Floyd's comrades, as related in their journal entries, is palpable. This was apparently the first time on the expedition that the men actually feared for the life of one of their party. "Bilious colic" was a common term used during that time to describe intestinal maladies. A common treatment for it and other illnesses was purging and bleeding. Whether the captains did this in an attempt to give Floyd relief is uncertain. If they did, it probably only hastened his death. If Floyd was suffering from an infected or ruptured appendix, laxatives would have worsened his condition. Bleeding him would have deprived him of desperately needed red and white blood cells to carry oxygen and fight infection, respectively. It also would have lowered his blood pressure. But even the best medical care back in Philadelphia would have followed this course of treatment. Clark does not record what vain attempts were made to help their comrade, but apparently nothing Lewis and Clark or the other men did helped.

During the night Floyd worsened to the point that Clark feared for his life. He stayed up most of the night with Floyd but could do nothing for the fast-sinking sergeant. "I am Dull & heavy," Clark wrote on 20 August, "been up the greater Part of last night with Serjt. Floyd, who is a[s] bad as he can be to live the [motion?] of his bowels having changed &c. &c. is the Cause of his violent attack &c. &c." When writing his fair copy of the journal, Clark noted that Floyd had "no pulse & nothing will Stay a moment on his Stomach or bowels —"[20]

Lewis and Clark and the other men were truly alarmed at Floyd's condition. About noon they put ashore for dinner and to "make a warm bath for Sergt. Floyd hopeing it would brace him a little." But he was past bracing or help of any kind: "before we could get him in to his bath he expired, with a great deal of composure, haveing Said to me before his death that he was going away and wished me to write a letter —"[21]

The captains had done everything they could for Floyd, and probably some things they shouldn't have. As already mentioned, if Floyd was indeed suffering from appendicitis and if the appendix was in danger of bursting or had burst, liberally dosing him with the strong laxative pills of Dr. Benjamin Rush (known as "Thunderclappers" because of their powerful purgative effect) would have only worsened his condition. But this was what Lewis had been trained to do and Clark would have concurred with what his partner administered. It was Whitehouse who specifically identified Lewis as the one prescribing medicine to the stricken sergeant. "The disease which occasion'd his death, was a Bilious cholic, which baffled all medical aid, that Captain Lewis could administer. . . ," he wrote. Gass, soon to be elected sergeant in Floyd's place, observed that Floyd died even though "every possible effort was made by the commanding officers, and other persons, to save his life."[22] But they could not, and on the afternoon of 20 August 1804 Sergeant Charles Floyd of the Corps of Discovery died, the first known American to die in the service of his country west of the Mississippi River.

Ordway, Whitehouse, and Gass also provide some information that Clark does not. Exactly where did Floyd die? All three wrote that after Floyd died, they proceeded on to hills on the north side of the river where he was buried. In his entry Clark wrote that they "took" Floyd's body, but then crossed it out and noted the burial ceremony and rites. This might indicate that they did move Floyd's body from where he actually died, but that Clark decided to only note the facts of the burial instead. Gass stated they traveled about one mile. Ordway wrote that they put to on the south (or west) side of the river. All three, as already mentioned, recorded proceeding to the north (or east) side to bury him. Clark is not specific about this, but seems to indicate the starboard (north or east) bank of the river as the one on which Floyd died. It might never definitely be known on which side of the Missouri Floyd died, but after he did, he "was laid out in the Best Manner possable" and then carried upstream to the first good hills, which were on the Iowa side, where his grave would be safe from floods and have a commanding view of the countryside.[23]

Clark, Ordway, and Whitehouse all provide some details regarding the burial of the fallen explorer. Whitehouse wrote that they "dug a Grave on the Top of a high round Nob; and Interred him, with all the honors of Warr. — and had a funeral Sermon preach'd over him." Ordway recorded that "we dug the Grave on a handsome Sightly Round knob close to the Bank. we buried him with the honours of war. the usal Serrymony performed (by Capt. Lewis[)] as custommary in a Settlement, we put a red ceeder post, hughn & branded his name date &.C —"[24]

Young Floyd's death was a blow to all the men. They had suffered the first loss among them. They undoubtedly wondered, Would this only be the first? Assuming Pryor kept a journal, his entries might have been particularly informative and touching, since he was not only Floyd's fellow sergeant and Kentuckian but also his first cousin. The Field brothers must have also keenly felt the loss. They had been together since the beginning and were possibly friends even before the expedition. Floyd's death certainly affected Clark. The family connection going back perhaps fifty years, knowing him before the expedition, and perhaps mentoring him as he grew into a soldier and leader on the journey would all have caused Clark to be deeply saddened by Floyd's passing. They had lost a member of the party who was truly one of his men, who had been with him since the start. His account of Floyd's illness, death, and burial is straightforward but obviously written with a great deal of feeling and sense of loss: "we buried him with all the honors of War, and fixed a Ceeder post at his head with his name title & Day of the month and year Capt Lewis read the funeral Service over him after paying every respect to the Body of this deceased man (who had at All times given us proofs of his impatiality Sincurity to ourselves and good will to Serve his Countrey) we returned to the Boat." Clark's fair copy entry for the day varies slightly from his field version: "he was buried with the Honors of War much lamented; a Seeder post with the (1) Name Sergt. C. Floyd died here 20th of August 1804 was fixed at the head of the grave— This Man at all times gave us proofs of his firmness and Deturmined resolution to doe Service to his Countrey and honor to himself after paying all the honor to our Deceed brother we Camped in the mouth of floyds river."[25]

What might have been the scene on top of that high hill with a commanding view of the countryside? The journals record that the explorers' deceased comrade was buried with all the honors of war, had a sermon preached over him, and had a funeral ceremony conducted by Lewis that was common in the settlements. We most likely will never know the details. But by using the basic statements of the journal keepers, it can be speculated what the scene might have been.

After Floyd died, he was no doubt washed and perhaps dressed in his best uniform, unless it was deemed best to keep it for others' use. He was wrapped in some available material for a shroud or maybe even placed in a crude coffin. Gass might have used his carpentry skills to hastily construct a coffin from available boards. If not, there is evidence that oak slabs placed along the inside of the grave and an oak plank or sawed timber placed on top as a lid served as a makeshift coffin.[26] The body was placed on the keelboat and taken to that prominent hill on the north side of the Missouri. A detachment was dispatched to the top to dig the grave. At the landing a procession was arranged and at a signal they solemnly advanced with the body of their fallen comrade. Once at the grave, the men formed ranks beside it and Floyd was lowered in. A mix of military and civilian services apparently followed. Lewis and Clark, as well as some of the other men, would have been familiar with the procedures of a military funeral. All of the men had almost certainly attended at least a general funeral service.

Captain Lewis officiated. Clark's reporting that Lewis read the funeral service over Floyd indicates that there would have been a reading from the Bible or perhaps the Episcopal *Book of Common Prayer*. There is no evidence that either book was carried on the expedition, but it is certainly possible, if not likely, that someone had at least carried a Bible with them on their wilderness journey. Lewis and perhaps Clark would have delivered a short sermon and paid tribute to Floyd and the service he had rendered to his country and the expedition. A hymn might have been sung. The honors of war would have included the firing of three volleys. The grave was then filled in and a cedar post branded "Sergt. C. Floyd—died here 20th of August 1804" was placed at the grave's head as a marker and a memorial to this "young man of much merit." The men then filed down the hill in the late afternoon heat, boarded their boats, and "proceeded on" to the mouth of a small river where they camped that "butifull evening," each with their own thoughts of their dead comrade, their own mortality, and what might lay ahead for them. In honor of Floyd the captains named the hill where he was buried Sergeant Floyd's Bluff and the river where they camped that night Floyd's River.[27]

And what of the letter that the dying sergeant asked his captain to write for him before he went "away"? Did Clark add his own words to those of Floyd in the letter? Was there time to write the letter before he died? And if it was written, did it find its way to Floyd's family? That might never be known. If it was written, it likely did reach the Floyds. Other letters written to friends, family, and officials were safely delivered. Clark quite possibly penned his own letter to Floyd's family, especially since he knew them. The family had definitely received word of the death of their "dear Charles" by the late spring of 1805—and probably before then. Newspapers carried news of it by early June 1805. Although they mourned his death they took comfort in knowing that "He was well cared for, as Clark was there."[28]

The next day the Corps continued their daily struggle up the river, toward their confrontation with the Teton Sioux, meeting with the Arikara, and winter stay among the Mandan and the Hidatsa. Some of Floyd's personal effects might have been saved for return to his family. It is believed that his journal was sent back down the Missouri in the spring of 1805. Lewis noted in his 7 April 1805 letter to Thomas Jefferson that "I have sent a journal kept by one of the Sergeants, to Capt. Stoddard, my agent at St. Louis, in order as much as possible to multiply the chances of saving something."[29] This seems to indicate that Stoddard or someone else in St. Louis held Floyd's journal until Lewis returned. If so, did Lewis then carry it to Kentucky on his return eastward to present to the late sergeant's family? Or did he keep it to use in preparing his own planned account of the expedition? If the latter, perhaps possession ultimately devolved to Clark after Lewis's death. Floyd's tomahawk remained with the Corps. On 2 June 1806, while among the Nez Perce Indians, Lewis recorded in his journal that an Indian stole Floyd's tomahawk and then sold it to another Indian. The explorers wanted this "prized" item back and tried to buy it from that Indian, but he was on the point of death and his family wanted to bury it with him. George Drouillard and two Nez Perces conducted the negotiations for the tomahawk's return. The family was finally persuaded to sell it, but they sold it dear, receiving a handkerchief and two strands of beads from the Corps' supply of goods and two horses from the chiefs. "Capt. C. was desirous of returning it to his friends," Lewis wrote.[30] Whether it was is uncertain.

By late summer of 1806 the Corps had dropped off the Charbonneau family at the Mandan–Hidatsa villages and said good-bye to Kentuckian John Colter, who had received permission to return westward. They were in a hurry to reach home, as they sped down the Missouri River, but they did not neglect to visit their fallen comrade. On 4 September, Clark recorded that he, Lewis, and several men walked to the top of Floyd's Bluff to visit his grave. There they "found the grave had been opened by the nativs and left half Covered." They filled the grave up again, said a final good-bye to Sergeant Floyd, and continued homeward.[31] Floyd was still in Clark's thoughts on 23 September, when he wrote his famous letter to his brother Jonathan Clark announcing the Corps' successful return. In wrapping up the lengthy report— intended for publication in order to circulate the news of their return—Clark noted that "we have not lost a man Since we left the mandans . . . which I assure you is a pleasing consideration to me."[32]

After the expedition's return, its members scattered. A few made names for themselves but most returned to the anonymity from which they had come before the journey. The fates of some remain unknown to this day. The grave sites of only a handful are known, and only a few are actually marked. Charles Floyd's is one of them. Ironically, the grave of the only man to die on the expedition is marked by a monument larger than that for any other member of the Corps, including Lewis and Clark. But such a tribute was not a sure thing. Just as fate intervened in preventing Floyd from completing his journey of discovery, it also intervened in saving his final resting place from being lost.

In the years following the expedition, Floyd's grave, with its cedar post reaching skyward, became a landmark on the Missouri. Travelers keeping written accounts of their journey on the Big Muddy often noted it. Both John Bradbury and Henry Brackenridge noted it while ascending the river in 1811. Brackenridge was particularly touched by the scene and mourned this "Brave, adventurous youth!" No known drawing of his grave was made until 1832. In that year the famous artist George Catlin stopped at the grave and sketched "this solitary cedar-post, which tells a tale of grief." Continuing, he wrote "'Floyd's Grave' is a name given to one of the most lovely and imposing mounds or bluffs on the Missouri River. . . . We encamped a couple of days at its base. I several times ascended it and sat upon the grave, overgrown with grass and the most delicate wild flowers, . . . and beheld from its top, the windings infinite of the Missouri, and its thousand hills and domes of green, vanishing into blue in distance."[33]

Given Catlin's eye for detail and commitment to accuracy, his painting entitled "Floyd's Grave" most likely can be relied upon as what was seen by those passing it in the first half of the nineteenth century. From the time of his death until the encroachment of the dynamic Missouri half a century later, Catlin's painting of Floyd's resting place provides a window into the past allowing us to see the young Kentuckian's grave as the Corps of Discovery and countless others saw it.

In May 1839 the eminent scientific explorer Joseph N. Nicollet, accompanied by young Lieutenant John C. Fremont, visited Floyd's grave while exploring the area for the U.S. Topographical Engineers. He noted in his expedition report that his men replaced the signal (cedar post) blown down by winds.[34] It is not clear whether they "replaced" it as in putting it back up or erecting a new one. It is likely that they simply put the post back up. One also wonders that having stood for some thirty years, if it is possible that vandals rather than wind pushed it over. It is impossible to know whether it was the original post. Six years before Nicollet visited, when Prince Maximilian and party ascended the Missouri, he noted that "a short stick marks the place where he [Floyd] is laid, and has often been renewed by travellers when the fires in the prairie have destroyed it."[35]

Eighteen years after Nicollet's visit, the shifting waters of the Missouri forever disturbed Floyd's resting place. The highway that had carried the Corps of Discovery into the heart of the West, served as the means for travelers to visit Floyd's grave, and been a constant beneath the bluff entombing the sergeant's remains now initiated a series of events that helped lead to a revived interest in the Lewis and Clark Expedition and the building of a memorial to the explorer. In the spring of 1857, during one of its common spring floods, the Missouri undermined Floyd's Bluff, sending part of it tumbling into its waters. The bluff was carried away to the point of Floyd's grave, almost sixty perpendicular feet above the river. The post marking the grave and a number of bones possibly fell into the river and were carried away. M. L. Jones of Smithland, Iowa, stated in 1895 that he was familiar with the grave and passed it frequently in 1854 and 1855, and that late in the fall of 1856 he noticed that the post, which had been almost intact, had been cut away almost to ground level.

Then, in late April 1857, while traveling from Sioux City home to Smithland, Jones recalled he noticed that the swollen river was cutting into the bluff and that the post and grave, which had been about one hundred feet from the edge of the bluff, appeared gone. A closer examination confirmed the post being gone and revealed bones protruding from the bank. Word was sent to Sioux City, and a party secured what was left of the bones the next day.[36]

Other accounts of the 1857 rescue of Floyd's remains offer additional and also contradictory information. Two statements refer to the coffin protruding from the collapsed bank, rather than oak slabs around the grave's sides and a board on top, over Floyd. Dr. S. P. Yeomans recollected in 1895 that a rope was tied around a man's waist and he was lowered over the edge of the bank to secure a cable to the box so that it could be raised to safety.[37]

Judge Noah Levering recalled that same year that in March 1857 it was discovered that the grave was being washed away and a rescue committee gathered up the skull and other bones they found for reburial at a safer spot. It was Levering who noted the oak slab construction of the "coffin" and that the "red" cedar post—that he remembered as having been whittled down to walking-stick size by souvenir hunters—had slid into the river. Six years later, in May 1901, Levering provided additional information. He recalled that Dr. Sloan of Sergeant Bluff, not M. L. Jones, discovered the danger to the grave, and when the rescue committee visited the site the next day, they observed a leg bone protruding from the ground. A young man volunteered to crawl to the edge while the committee held a rope tied around his waist, and using a spade he dug out bones and pieces of the makeshift coffin. Levering carried the bones home but his wife did not like them about the house, so he gave them to Judge Marshall F. Moore for safekeeping. In May 1857 the remains were placed in a new coffin, carried by the ferryboat *Lewis Burns* to the bluff, and re-interred in a patriotic and religious ceremony some six hundred feet further back from the edge of the bluff with head- and footboards to mark the grave site. Levering thought the post that had slid into the river was probably the third one to mark the grave, placed there by Nicollet, he surmised. A couple of days after recalling these events, he stated that no bones were lost to the encroachment of the river. Any bones that were missing were due to wild animals disturbing the grave, as early visitors had reported.[38]

Almost forty years would pass before the remains of Sergeant Floyd and his grave would again become the focus of attention. Like a phoenix rising from the ashes, it was Floyd's own journal, kept during his fateful journey up the Missouri in 1804 that provided the spark for a movement that culminated in a monument honoring him.

On 3 February 1893, while at the State Historical Society of Wisconsin examining a pile of notebooks written by that voracious collector of early western manuscripts Lyman C. Draper, Reuben Gold Thwaites discovered Floyd's journal. How Draper acquired the journal is uncertain, but once he did, it disappeared into his vast collection, there to lay for some thirty to fifty years until Thwaites found it. Professor James D. Butler of Madison, Wisconsin, learned of the journal and presented a paper on it to the American Antiquarian Society in April 1894. The American Antiquarian Society subsequently published both Butler's paper and Floyd's journal. These events, together with the publication of Elliott Coues's edition of the Lewis and Clark journals, stirred new interest in the expedition. This was particularly true in the Sioux City area, where interest was rekindled in Floyd's life, his death, and his grave.[39]

Area newspapers, especially the *Sioux City Journal*, carried articles regarding Floyd and his grave and the possibility of erecting a monument honoring him. There had been discussion of a monument in 1857 at the time of the rescue and reinterment of his remains but nothing came of it. Although building a monument to the young sergeant might never have faded entirely from the minds of those who remembered the 1857 reburial, the events of 1893 and 1894 proved to be the catalyst that achieved results.[40]

An association was proposed by interested Iowans in the Sioux City area in 1895 to finally honor Floyd with a monument. Detailed coverage of the plans by the *Sioux City Journal* helped stimulate public interest and support for the endeavor. Some of these articles were picked up by the Associated Press and, together with letters of support in national publications written by Elliott Coues, the plan for an association was realized. The date 20 August 1895 was set as the date for a suitable ceremony to again rebury Sergeant Floyd's remains and to incorporate the Floyd Memorial Association. This time, unlike thirty-eight years earlier, a proper marker would be placed over the grave until a more substantial monument could be constructed.[41]

There was one problem: the grave could not be found! In the years since the 1857 reburial, the head and foot markers of the grave had been broken off and their remains were beneath ground level. Already in the winter of 1867, engineer Mitchell Vincent, of Onawa, Iowa, had reported the only visible sign of the grave to be a shallow six-inch depression extending perhaps two feet by one foot. Mitchell was conducting railroad work on the bluff at the time and instructed the crew to respect the grave. He recalled that he would have liked to have formed at least a mound over the grave, but the ground being frozen prevented him from doing so. When spring arrived, his good intentions were forgotten and Floyd's grave continued a silent, neglected witness to the water, rail, and road traffic passing by. As the years passed, less and less remained of the grave to identify it, and by 1895 there was no obvious sign of it left.[42]

An attempt early in 1895 to locate the grave failed. The consternation caused by this situation helped stiffen the resolve of the leaders of the memorial movement. Many of them were early residents of the area. Among themselves and with the help of other old settlers, many of whom attended the 1857 reburial, another attempt was made on Memorial Day, 30 May 1895. This search met with success. Using faded memories, partly confused from the changed appearance of the bluff, and a more scientific method of probing for color differences in the soil, the grave was found. Desiring other witnesses to be on hand for the exhumation, especially those who had been at the 1857 ceremonies, further digging was delayed until 6 June. Digging on that day revealed several inches below the surface the remains of the oak head and footboards placed there in 1857. Going deeper, the moldering wood of the coffin was uncovered. A spade thrust through its rotted top revealed the skull and other bones. The identification was declared successful! Optimism for their monument project was high, and right there on the spot the Floyd Memorial Association was formed.

Upon reflection, the original intention to leave the grave undisturbed was reconsidered. It was decided to remove the skull to town for safekeeping and then recover the grave. There would be no forgetting Floyd's grave again. The *Journal* covered the activities and founding of the Association, and plans immediately were made for reburial ceremonies on the same site for 20 August, the ninety-first anniversary of the sergeant's death.[43]

Over the next three months the Association met regularly and made all necessary arrangements for the 20 August ceremonies. Mitchell Vincent platted the bluff and determined that Floyd's 1804 grave was now 100 feet in the air over the Missouri, and that the 1857 grave was about 360 feet from the solid edge of the railroad cut on the western side of the bluff. When erosion of the bank, the railroad cut, and the present site of the grave all were factored together, Vincent determined that the 1857 grave was southeast from the original one by about 600 feet.[44]

At the Association's 24 June meeting, John H. Charles was elected president, a position he would hold until a monument to Floyd towered over the Iowa prairie six years later. A monument was very important to Charles, and he worked diligently toward achieving that end. Committees were formed at the meeting with the duties of inviting Coues and Butler to be speakers at the 20 August ceremonies, acquiring the land containing the grave for a park, and procuring a suitable receptacle for Floyd's bones and a proper stone to temporarily mark the grave.

On 6 July, photographs of Floyd's skull and the vicinity of the original grave were exhibited at a meeting of the executive committee. The photographer, at least of the grave view, was P. C. Waltermire of Sioux City. His services were retained for the reburial and monument exercises. Thanks to him and his camera, there are photographs of the 1895, 1900, and 1901 ceremonies. It was also decided at this meeting that a marble slab seven feet by three feet and eight inches thick, properly inscribed, would be ordered at a cost of $40, and that a pottery urn would be made to hold the bones. Coues's recommendation that Floyd's skull be given to a historical repository was declined, but two plaster casts of it were made, one of which was given to the Iowa Historical Society.[45]

The day for the reburial ceremonies was fast approaching, and all the arrangements were coming together, from the slab to the train to carry the expected crowd. A detailed schedule of the afternoon and evening programs was approved, and articles of incorporation for the Association were drafted and ready for adoption.

The anticipated day dawned bright and warm. The train departed for Floyd's Bluff at 1:45 that afternoon, fifteen minutes behind schedule, crowded with some four

The reburial of Sergeant Charles Floyd, 20 August 1895. The two urns contain his remains. James Butler is seated in the center holding Floyd's journal. Credit: The Filson Historical Society

hundred passengers. An additional one hundred spectators took other conveyances. From the base of the bluff the procession was led to the top by the General Hancock Post, No. 22, Grand Army of the Republic, with fife and drum playing. Old settlers, Association officers, speakers, city and county officials, appropriate others, and the attendees followed in that order. The Association had prepared the grave site before 20 August. The other bones had been exhumed, and they and the skull placed in two earthenware urns. The crowd viewed the urns, and then President Charles, acting as master of ceremonies, opened the program. Judge George W. Wakefield, speaking on behalf of Sioux City, made a brief address. Professor Butler, who delivered the funeral oration, followed him. In place of a Bible, Butler held the original Floyd journal. After his address recalling that sad day ninety-one years earlier, Congressman George Perkins representing the Iowa Historical Society, General Hancock Post Commander Eugene Rice, the Reverend H. D. Jenkins, Coues, and Dr. S. P. Yeomans all delivered short speeches.

The crowd then gathered around the open grave for photographs. The two urns were lowered into the grave, a wreath and flowers were placed on them, and the grave was then filled in. The inscribed stone was laid over it; the articles of incorporation

The Floyd grave site with marble marker following the 20 August 1895 reburial. The grave remained like this until the 1900 reburial of Floyd's remains in the base of the monument. Credit: The Filson Historical Society

of the Floyd Memorial Association were signed beside it; and Rev. Jenkins closed the bluff-top ceremonies with a benediction.

At eight o'clock the evening program began at the Sioux City YMCA auditorium. The main speaker was Dr. Coues, and after a few preliminaries the Lewis and Clark scholar spoke on the expedition. Professor Butler followed, speaking on Charles Floyd and again displaying his original journal.[46]

Now that the immediate goal of a permanent marker for Floyd's grave had been achieved, the Association began looking toward its ultimate goal of erecting a monument to the fallen expedition member. Local residents were the leaders of the Association and formed the majority of the membership, but interested people from across the country also joined. Coues and Butler belonged for obvious reasons, and even served as vice presidents. Another four of the fifteen vice presidents were descendants of William Clark. These tended to be honorary positions, with the exception of Coues, who wrote the excellent 1897 report of the Association.[47]

Over the next several years the board of the Association, and primarily the executive committee, worked toward making a monument to the lone fatality of the Corps of Discovery a reality. At the 20 August 1898 annual meeting of the Association, it was reported that one acre of ground surrounding Floyd's grave had been fenced and planted with trees, and that a monument of the type researched (a shaft) would cost $6,000 to $10,000 depending on the material used.[48]

By the time of the 1899 annual meeting, a $5,000 appropriation from Congress had been secured; final negotiations were under way for the purchase of twenty-one bluff-top acres surrounding Floyd's grave site for a park; and discussions were being held with the Sioux City office of the U.S. Army Corps of Engineers regarding the planning and construction of a monument. No definite plan had been decided on, but approval was given to John Charles's motion to proceed with a seventy-five-foot shaft of Sioux Falls quartzite, to be ready for dedication on 20 August 1900.[49] This plan proved premature, and discussion continued with the Corps of Engineers.

The end of the century whose beginning had witnessed the Lewis and Clark Expedition proved to be the stage upon which a monument to Charles Floyd would become a reality. By May 1900 enough money had been raised to proceed with the monument plans designed by Captain Hiram M. Chittenden of the Corps of Engineers. In April the State of Iowa had matched a congressional appropriation of $5,000 for a monument. At the 9 May meeting of the executive committee, Chittenden's plan was approved. His design was an Egyptian obelisk. His predecessor, Captain James C. Sanford, had recommended the same style of monument. Chittenden had thoroughly studied the matter upon assuming supervision of the Sioux City office, and reached the same conclusion. In a letter dated 26 January 1900, he stated that the "character of the site, . . . as the purposes of the work, require a monument which shall be imposing in appearance, and visible at a great distance, dominating the entire valley in its vicinity, rather than an example of fine artistic work, whose merits, to be appreciated, must be examined close by." To this end, the Egyptian obelisk was the best choice. He also listed the types of stone—granite, limestone, and sandstone—that could be used. The captain stated that all were suitable, and while granite was the preferred stone, it was likely sandstone would be used because of cost restrictions. Chittenden was correct. A couple of months later Kettle River sandstone from a quarry in Minnesota was selected. Although they were cost conscious, the Association's executive committee and Chittenden insisted that all materials and workmanship be of good quality. The Association's reports and Chittenden's 1901 report to the chief of engineers testify to this.[50]

By late May 1900 the plans, finances, and ceremony arrangements were all in place. The next step in the monument project was at hand—pouring the foundation, to be followed several months later, after it had set, by the obelisk. All was in readiness for the morning of 29 May. Chittenden assembled 110 men early that morning who had been hired for the day so that he could maintain more direct control over the project.

Laying of the Floyd Monument cornerstone, 20 August 1900. Credit: The Filson Historical Society

They were government workers doing river work and Sioux City street workers. With the planning and preparation of a military operation, they all were briefed on the project and assigned their duties.

The force left the railroad station at seven o'clock, and half an hour later the first concrete was poured. Everything needed had already been assembled or was hauled in during the day to keep the work progressing. This was extremely important because the foundation had to be poured in one day to assure that it would set as one solid mass. And a solid mass it was! Measuring twenty-two-feet square at the base, fourteen-feet square at the top, and eleven-feet high, with thirty-two heavy steel rails interlaced through it, the foundation required 138.6 cubic yards of concrete and weighed some two hundred tons. A mechanical mixer was deemed unnecessary and the concrete was mixed by hand. As wheelbarrow after wheelbarrow of concrete ran up the ramps and deposited its load in the excavation that would become the foundation, the caisson around the work was built up, the ramps adjusted, and the supplies replenished. Chittenden and his assistant engineer, Bathurst Smith (whom Chittenden recognized as supervising much of the work on the project in his 1901 report), kept vigilant eyes on the work's progress. Chittenden had estimated ten hours for the project and he hit his mark almost exactly. The last shovel of concrete was deposited at 5:20, and by 6:00 the workers were headed home. It would now be only a few months before the stones began to rise skyward to memorialize Sergeant Floyd.[51]

Following its tradition, the Association chose 20 August to lay the cornerstone of the monument. It had been decided to transfer the sergeant's remains into the monument for permanent entombment there. Accordingly, they were exhumed yet again on the morning of 20 August and placed in the center of the foundation, ready to be covered with concrete during the afternoon ceremonies.

Just as they had done on 20 August 1895, the Association and citizens of Sioux City planned suitable ceremonies for the event. The heat and blazing sun caused some of the activities to be abandoned, but the main event—the laying of the cornerstone—would be carried out.

The parade in town to the station was abbreviated. The railroad cars, loaded with some 250 people, pulled out for the bluff just behind schedule. They were joined by hundreds of others at the grave site, and while the Fourth Regiment Band, better known as Reed's Band, played a quickstep, two companies of guardsmen led a scattered procession up the hill.

The Reverend J. C. McClintock offered a blessing on the proceedings just after two o'clock. George Perkins, speaking on behalf of the Iowa Historical Society, followed him. Perkins spoke on Floyd, his grave, and the Association. The Association's board of trustees was unanimously reelected (to take care of some necessary business), and then the mayor of Sioux City, A. H. Burton, placed a time capsule beside the urns in the center of the monument's base. Some sort of structure apparently housed these items, because a concrete top was then placed over them.

In a mixed military-religious ceremony conducted by the GAR Post and guardsmen, the cornerstone was laid. A final address was given and the band played "America." Just like Floyd's fellow explorers did for him ninety-six years earlier in presenting the honors of war to a fallen soldier, three volleys were fired in salute. The mournful sound of taps then drifted from the bluff to end the ceremony.[52]

Following the laying of the cornerstone, the Kettle River sandstone blocks were laid as they were delivered. The core of the monument was filled with concrete as new courses were laid. Delivery was slow, and by the end of October only sixteen courses had been laid. With the cold prairie winter approaching, Chittenden expressed doubts that the monument could be completed that year. He was right. On 18 November the Minnesota Sandstone Company delivered the last of the stone—four days after work had been suspended for the winter. When work was suspended on 14 November, the monument had risen to a height of fifty-five feet, just more than halfway to its planned one hundred feet. The new stone was carefully housed to wait for spring.

Plans for the spring completion of the monument proceeded during the winter. Contracts and work for the steel fence around the obelisk, the two bronze tablets to be set in the shaft, and grading, paving, and roadwork around the monument all were awarded or done.[53] Work on the monument resumed on 28 March 1901 and proceeded as rapidly as possible. The obelisk quickly rose higher despite delays caused by high winds. On 22 April the capstone of the obelisk was laid, completing the work on the shaft itself. Its final dimensions were a height of 100.174 feet, a base of 9.42 feet square, and a weight of 278 tons. Six sandstone blocks were used in each course. The shaft decreased by one-third from base to top. Related work continued after 22 April. The placement of the tablets on the east and west faces of the shaft, the roadway from the highway to the monument, and the steel fence were completed by late May in time for the Memorial Day dedication on 30 May. Only a little paving work around the monument remained to be done.[54]

Memorial Day 1901 in the Sioux City area was a most memorable one. The Floyd Memorial Association planned the ceremonies meticulously, wanting the day that would witness the culmination of years of effort to go perfectly. And perfect it was. The graves of Sioux City's soldiers were decorated with flags and flowers early that morning. At 10:15 a special train left for the monument. Once there its passengers joined those who had already arrived by other means.

Reminiscent of the scene that had been played out twice before, the participants and spectators gathered around the grave of Sergeant Floyd—a grave that had changed much in the past six years. New and old faces alike were among the crowd. President Charles and Professor Butler, again carrying the precious journal just as

Workers putting the finishing touches on the top of the monument, ca. 22 April 1901.
Credit: The Filson Historical Society

Dedication of the Floyd Monument, 30 May 1901. Credit: The Filson Historical Society

he had six years earlier, were there. Levering, who had played such an important role in the 1857 rescue of the remains, journeyed from Los Angeles for the occasion. The daughter of William Bratton, one of the "Nine Young Men from Kentucky," was there, as were many others. The crowd was estimated at two thousand. Patriotic music filled the air, courtesy of Reed's Band, while the dignitaries took seats and the crowd settled down in anticipation of the start of the hour-long ceremonies.

An invocation began the dedication, followed by a musical selection, and then Captain Chittenden reviewed the facts of the project that had resulted in this almost $20,000 monument surrounded by a twenty-one-acre park. He then officially offered the monument to the Floyd Memorial Association. Charles and vice president Wakefield accepted the monument with appropriate remarks. The bronze tablets were unveiled and a descendant of Thomas Jefferson spoke. The General Hancock Post then assumed control of the ceremonies and dedicated the monument to the memory of Sergeant Charles Floyd. Professor Butler offered a few remarks and displayed Floyd's journal. He compared it to the monument, saying it was the obelisk Floyd had erected and was his own enduring monument. Shortly before noon a bugler blew retreat, a three-volley salute from twenty-four guns was given, and taps sounded from the bluff as the crowd dispersed.

Afternoon ceremonies got under way at two o'clock. A parade by Civil War veterans, Sioux City companies of the Iowa National Guard, representatives of civic societies, and city officials ended at the Opera House, where people went inside for a three o'clock program. American flags and bunting decorated the interior of the Opera House and Reed's Band was again on hand to play patriotic songs. Other musical groups also participated during the program, singing songs suitable for a day set aside to honor America's warriors. After the invocation, a musical selection, and a reading of the Gettysburg Address, the Grand Army of the Republic's memorial service for the dead was performed. A tribute to President Charles moved the "well loved old man" to tears. Orator, diplomat, and politician, Iowa's own John A. Kasson was the main speaker. He spoke for about an hour on the Louisiana Purchase, Lewis and Clark, Floyd, the monument, and what it all signified. "America" closed the afternoon program.[55]

The day's celebration and monument dedication activities drew to a close that night at the Court House auditorium. Butler delivered the evening's address. Again displaying the journal, he recounted its importance and history, the Corps' and especially the captains' love for Floyd, a story of the sergeant's hatchet, and likened the journal to "the acorn from which an obelisk grander than any oak has grown." Longtime area resident and Association officer Yeomans spoke next, focusing on the monument, its significance, and its symbolism concerning U.S. history. Levering was recognized for his role in rescuing Floyd's remains and took the opportunity to correct an error concerning the state of those remains in 1857. Patriotic music was played and sung during the program, and that favorite, "America," closed the proceedings of that eventful Memorial Day.[56]

All that remained to totally complete the monument was some paving around the obelisk and the inevitable cleanup. Both were accomplished by late June, and on 30 June, Chittenden settled accounts and resigned as engineer for the Association.[57]

Thus was completed the dream of an enduring memorial to the only member of the Corps of Discovery to die on the expedition. The Floyd Memorial Association accomplished the erection of a monument larger and more impressive than any constructed for any other member of the Corps, including Lewis and Clark. It helped rescue Floyd from the near anonymity that has been the fate of most of the expedition's members. Ninety-seven years after a cedar post was erected to mark the grave of Sergeant Charles Floyd, a stone obelisk soared above the Missouri and surrounding prairie to mark his grave; a fitting monument indeed to this "young man of much merit."

The completed Floyd Monument looking across
the Missouri River from Nebraska, ca. 1901.
Credit: The Filson Historical Society

He sleeps beneath the stately shaft
    Beside the winding river,
Where prairie grasses clothe the sod
    And stunted willows quiver;
The waters murmur as they flow
In a requiem, softly, faintly low,
    And the west winds sigh and shiver.

No word can reach his earth-stopt ears
    However loudly spoken;
To words of praise, to words of blame
    His dust can give no token;
He holds his vigil on the hill,
In endless quiet, deep and still,
    In dignity unbroken.

Above his solemn resting place
    The meadowlarks are singing;
Around the stately obelisk
    The butterflies are winging;
With reverence and peace draw near
The grave of the sleeping pioneer
    While paeans of praise are ringing.

His restless feet have turned to dust,
    His wanderings are ended;
But still his spirit bides with us
    With courage high and splendid;
His strong example paved the way
For all the triumphs of today—
    His hopes on us descended.

He sleeps beneath the stately shaft
    Enwrapped in solemn glory;
Eternal hills lift up their heads
    About him, old and hoary;
And like a finger, pointing high,
The shaft lifts upward to the sky
    And tells its deathless story.

—Will Reed Dunroy[58]

The basis for this introduction is an article on the death of Charles Floyd and the history of his grave and monument written by the author and published in the August 1996 issue of We Proceeded On *magazine ("Monument to a 'Young Man of Much Merit'"). It has been expanded here to include an account of Floyd's life. Minor revisions have been made to the 1996 article.*

NOTES

1. Holmberg, ed., *Dear Brother*, pp. 17, 54 n; Jackson, 1: 57–60, 110–11.
2. Jackson, 1:58.
3. Jackson, 1:113, 117.
4. Jackson, 2:378.
5. Jackson, 1:366–67.
6. Kleber, p. 330. The Floyd and Clark families had known each other for years. Floyds had served in the militia under George Rogers Clark. They also lived in the same neighborhood along Beargrass Creek—the Floyds along the Middle Fork and the Clarks along the South Fork.
7. Mordy, pp. 3, 13–18, 28–29; Kleber, p. 330; Yater, pp. 4–5. Floyd family descendant Anna Margaret Cartlidge researched and wrote an unpublished manuscript in 1966 entitled "Children and Grand-children of William and Abadiah (Davis) Floyd." James C. Mordy (also a Floyd family descendant) used it as a major source for his paper. The documentation cited by Cartlidge, Mordy, and other historians in recent years clearly establishes Charles Floyd's father to be Robert and not Charles Floyd (who is actually his uncle), as is generally cited in Lewis and Clark histories. Other speculation has centered on whether the Clarks and the Floyds were related, since Robert bore the middle name of Clark. No familial connection has been determined but both lived in Albemarle County, Virginia, at the same time. It is quite possible that the families were neighbors and friends. At the very least, they would have known each other. Both Robert Floyd and George Rogers Clark were born in Albemarle in 1752. Perhaps Robert received his middle name as a mark of friendship between the families.
8. Yater, p. 5; Mordy, pp. 3, 13. Charles Floyd's contract paid $600 annually, $50 more than the standard contract because of the hardship and danger of the route.
9. Mordy, p. 3; Appleman, "Joseph and Reubin Field," p. 21; Yater, pp. 3–6; Holmberg, pp. 93 n–96 n. For more information on expedition events in Kentucky and particularly at the Falls of the Ohio in 1803, see Holmberg, "Kentucky and the Lewis & Clark Expedition," pp. 5–17, 42–44, 46–47.
10. Camp Dubois, also called Camp River a Dubois or Wood River, was established near the mouth of that river and the Mississippi. The exact location of the camp is debated today, and studies are being done to try to locate it. For a discussion of the Corps' timeline in ascending the Mississippi and the Spanish refusal to allow the Americans to venture up the Missouri until they officially relinquished control of Upper Louisiana, see the pertinent notes for Clark's letter to his brother, Jonathan Clark, dated 16 December 1803, in Holmberg, ed., *Dear Brother*, pp. 65 n–75 n.
11. Holmberg, p. 62; Moulton, 2:134, 137, 175, 176 n, 193, 205.
12. Moulton, *Journals of the Lewis and Clark Expedition*, 2:139. (Note: All subsequent Moulton citations in these notes refer to this multivolume work unless otherwise noted.)
13. Moulton, 2:179, 188–89.
14. Moulton, 2:244.
15. Moulton, 2:254–58.
16. Moulton, 2:256–57.
17. Moulton, 2:257–58.
18. Moulton, 2:429; 9:32–33, 391. Volume nine of the Moulton edition consists of the journals of both Ordway and Floyd.
19. Moulton, 2:492. For a comparison of what Ordway, Gass, and Whitehouse wrote see Moulton, 9:41; 10:28–29; 11:58. Volume ten is Gass's journal and eleven is Whitehouse's.
20. Moulton, 2:494–95.
21. Moulton, 2:495. In Clark's fair copy journal he actually quotes Floyd, writing, "he Said to me, 'I am going away' [']I want you to write me a letter'—" Ordway and Whitehouse both gave the time as noon. Gass recorded it as being about two in the afternoon. Moulton, 9:41; 10:29; 11:58. None of the other diarists mention a bath. Will the specific cause of Floyd's death ever be determined? It seems doubtful. A number of medical professionals have investigated his death, using the symptoms of his fatal illness described in the journals, and failed to specifically determine the cause. There are various theories as to the malady that killed Floyd. The best evidence indicates appendicitis resulting in a rup-tured appendix and peritonitis. An intestinal infection and tularemia have also been proposed as possible causes. For more information, see these books by three medical doctors: Chuinard, *Only One Man Died: The Medical Aspects of the Lewis and Clark Expedition;* Paton, *Lewis & Clark: Doctors in the Wilderness;* and Peck, *"Or Perish in the Attempt": Wilderness Medicine on the Lewis & Clark Expedi-tion.* Chuinard supports appendicitis/ruptured appendix and Paton an intestinal infection. Peck discusses a variety of possibilities, including a stom-ach ulcer and a bacterial infection called tularemia, but seems to favor appendicitis/ruptured appendix as perhaps the best possibility.
22. Moulton, 10:29; 11:58. In reading Gass's journal entries for the following days, it is interesting to note that he made no mention of being elected sergeant in place of the deceased Floyd. It is possible that he did, but that David McKeehan, the editor of Gass's now lost original journal, deleted it.
23. Moulton, 2:495; 9:41; 10:29; 11:58. The party often camped and stopped on the south or west side of the river, so there is nothing unusual about them stop-ping on that side on the afternoon of 20 August. Also, Ordway in his journal consistently uses S.S. (south

side) and N.S. (north side) to denote the sides of
the river. He does not appear to use S. to refer to the
starboard or right side as Lewis and Clark often do.
Therefore, if Ordway is interpreted correctly, and he
recorded correctly what bank of the river they were
on, Floyd actually died on the Nebraska side and was
buried about one mile (according to Gass) upstream
on the Iowa side inside the present city limits of
Sioux City. If Clark is correct in writing that they
put to on the starboard, or north/east bank, then
Floyd died in Iowa. Either way, Floyd is believed to
be the first United States serviceman to die west of
the Mississippi River.

24. Moulton, 9:41; 11:58. Ordway's, Gass's, and Whitehouse's journal entries for Floyd's illness, death,
being laid out, and burial are quite similar, if not
essentially the same, and might be an example of
them copying from each other or writing by committee. If the former, Ordway was probably the
primary author.

25. Moulton, 2:495.

26. Coues, *In Memoriam, Sergeant Charles Floyd;*
pp. 14–16; Floyd Memorial Association, p. 103. Elliott
Coues's 1895 report on Charles Floyd, prepared on
behalf of the Floyd Memorial Association, and the
Association's second report, published in 1901, are
the two best sources for a detailed history of Floyd's
grave and monument.

27. Moulton, 2:495; Hunt, pp. 10–15. Robert R. Hunt
provides a good description of what the funeral might
have been like, combining the military, civilian, and
Masonic aspects of early nineteenth-century funeral
practice. The funeral service definitely followed military ritual in part, as the journalists noted. Although
they were not known to be particularly religious,
Lewis and Clark were both Episcopalians and would
have been familiar with that denomination's funeral
service. Other members of the Corps undoubtedly
also had Episcopal roots, as well as those of other
denominations, such as Methodism and Presbyterian-
ism, to whom reading the Bible and perhaps carrying one with them was important. It is known that
the Clark family owned Bibles. The Bible was a major
source for reading. Lewis was also an active Mason
and might have used some of that order's funeral
rituals. Thus Floyd's funeral might have been something of a mix of military, civilian, and Masonic.
That same issue of *We Proceeded On* also includes
short illustrated articles by the late Strode Hinds
on the project to create a likeness of Floyd using
forensic science and by facial reconstruction artist
Sharon Long about creating the bust. Today the
site of Floyd's grave is named Sergeant Bluff and
the river Floyd River. The former is still commonly
called Floyd's Bluff.

28. Yater, p. 6; Jackson, 1:370; *The Western Spy,* 26 June
1805 and 3 July 1805. Published in Cincinnati, the
paper carried a 5 June report from Vincennes, Indiana Territory, and an 8 June report from Frankfort,
Kentucky. Both reported a man dying on the journey.
The Vincennes report gave Charles Floyd's name.

29. Jackson, 1:232.

30. Moulton, 7:326.

31. Moulton, 8:349. In 1810, Clark added a degree of
mystery and confusion to Floyd's grave site. In that
year, during one of his interviews with Nicholas
Biddle concerning the latter's preparation of the
captains' journals for publication, he told Biddle that
a Sioux chief had opened Floyd's grave and buried
his son with the sergeant. His reason for doing that
was so his son could accompany the white man to
the other world, because the whites' future state was
thought to be happier than that of the Indians. When
this addition of a body to Floyd's grave occurred—
if it actually did occur—is uncertain. It would seem
that if the Corps had discovered another body in
Floyd's grave in 1806, they would have made note of
it. They did not. Therefore, a more likely explanation
is that some time between September 1806 and the
summer of 1809, when Clark left St. Louis for the
East, he heard this information and subsequently
passed it on to Biddle about April of 1810. There is
no mention of a second set of remains in the Floyd
Memorial Association reports. The story Clark
related to Biddle has a certain apocryphal ring to it
and seems unlikely. See Moulton, 9:349 n–350 n; and
Jackson, 2:541–42.

32. Holmberg, *Dear Brother,* p. 106; Jackson, 1:329.

33. Coues, *In Memoriam,* pp. 12–13; Thwaites, ed., *Early
Western Travels, 1748–1846,* 5:91; 6:85; Catlin, 2:3–5.
The illustration of "Floyd's Grave" is opposite p. 3.
While George Catlin's prose is rather florid, he still
provides a good firsthand account of Floyd's grave.
The original edition of Catlin's *Letters and Notes* was
published in 1841 and went through a number of
editions. "Floyd's Grave" is Plate 118 in the original
edition.

34. Coues, *In Memoriam,* pp. 13–14; Thwaites, ed., *Early
Western Travels, 1748–1846,* 22:278. For a full report
of Joseph N. Nicollet's expedition, see *Senate Document No. 237,* 26th Congress, 2nd Session (February
1841); and *House Document No. 52,* 28th Congress,
2nd Session (11 January 1845). They were published in
1843 and 1845, respectively. Nicollet also was known
as Jean rather than Joseph.

35. Coues, *In Memoriam,* pp. 14–15.

36. Coues, *In Memoriam,* pp. 15–16. M. L. Jones's description would indicate that either Floyd had been buried
with his head toward the river or the post had been
relocated to the foot of the grave at some time if the
post was gone and bones were protruding from the
bank. Clark was very specific in stating that they
placed the cedar post at the head of Floyd's grave.

37. Coues, *In Memoriam,* pp. 15–16.

38. Coues, *In Memoriam,* pp. 16–18; Floyd Memorial
Association, pp. 90, 103–4; *The Sioux City Sunday
Journal,* 26 November 1950, p. 1. There are a number
of contradictions in the accounts of the 1857 rescue.
The account of Noah Levering, who initially was
involved with the project, appears to be the most
reliable. He does not mention certain facts, however,
and makes some contradictory statements. The bones
of the lower body were recovered, indicating that
Floyd was buried with his head to the river. If the post

and upper bones of the body were washed away, why not the skull? Coues surmised in his report that the skull, collarbone, and some rib fragments were gathered later from where they had been scattered down the bluff. Levering stated that he gave a piece of the original "coffin" to the Iowa Historical Society. He also stated in his 1901 letter that he believed the cedar post washed away in 1857 was not the one erected by the Corps of Discovery, but rather the third one and that it probably was placed there by Nicollet in 1839. He thought Nicollet did not know exactly where the body lay and placed the post at Floyd's feet. Levering was mistaken in believing this. A post at Floyd's feet would mean that the lower bones of the body rather than the upper ones would have fallen down the bank. There is never a mention of the possibility of more than one body being in the grave, as Clark stated to Biddle in 1810. In his remarks at the 1901 dedication, Levering, apparently after further reflection, stated that no bones were lost to the river, but that wild animals had carried off those that were missing. This theory could be closest to the truth, but it will probably never be definitely known. The piece of "coffin" as well as one of Floyd's teeth is in the collection of the State Historical Society of Iowa, Iowa City branch.

39. Butler, pp. 229–31; "The Floyd Obelisk," *The Nation*, pp. 471–72. Lyman C. Draper was the longtime secretary of the State Historical Society of Wisconsin. Reuben Gold Thwaites was his successor. James Davie Butler had an interest in the Trans-Mississippi West and by his own account had known Draper for some forty years. Draper "scoured every corner of Kentucky . . . to beg, borrow, buy or steal ancient documents," Butler remembered, but once he had them locked behind the iron door of his fireproof building he lost interest in them, focusing instead on new collections to acquire. He collected in Kentucky, Missouri, Tennessee, Virginia, and other states for some fifty years, with his most successful period being the 1840s and 1850s. Butler is correct concerning Draper's method of collecting documents, though he perhaps did not outright "steal" papers. He often would "borrow" those documents he could not buy or be given, and then fail to return them. When families sought the return of their family papers, he generally avoided them, delayed, or simply did not answer their letters (which is how most families requested their return). Families today still refer to that "pirate" Draper making off with their loaned family papers and refusing to return them.

Although it is not certain how Draper acquired Floyd's journal, there are several possibilities. Reuben T. Durrett, founder of The Filson Club (now The Filson Historical Society) and a noted collector himself, theorized that Draper got it from the Floyd family or possibly the William Croghan family, both of the Louisville area. Butler and Coues apparently subscribed to this theory. Croghan was William Clark's brother-in-law. William's brother, and Draper's frontier hero, George Rogers Clark, lived at the home of William and Lucy Clark Croghan the last nine years of his life. Draper acquired a large collection of George Rogers Clark papers, in addition to Croghan papers, from the Croghans's son, Dr. John Croghan, in the 1840s. It is quite possible that among those papers was Floyd's journal. Another possibility is that the journal was contained in the papers that Draper borrowed from Jonathan Clark's son Isaac and never returned. The materials being sent to Louisville in the spring of 1805 were sent to Clark's oldest brother, Jonathan. They included Clark's famous "Field Notes." If William never retrieved the journal from Jonathan's papers, it may have been included in the batch of Jonathan, George Rogers, and William Clark papers that Isaac lent to Draper. This possibility would seem to be disproved, however, by Lewis's statement to Jefferson that he was sending a sergeant's journal (almost certainly Floyd's) to Amos Stoddard to hold for him. It might have eventually ended up with William Clark or been included for some reason in Clark's shipment of papers and artifacts to Jonathan.

An additional piece of evidence to be considered is the placement of Floyd's journal in the Draper Manuscripts. When found among Draper's papers in 1893, Thwaites and his staff at Wisconsin Historical were processing and cataloging Draper's manuscript collection. There is no known record of what specific papers comprised that stack in which the Floyd journal was found. It also is not known if the papers in that stack would have reflected their provenance or had been reordered to some extent by Draper. It was Thwaites and society staff who arranged and described the collection, which included imposing a numbering system. Draper's order was retained when possible. New categories (or series) were created and papers interfiled in existing ones as necessary. How the Floyd journal was handled is a mystery. It was cataloged as 6M. The papers in the series are almost entirely those of William Clark, a cousin of the explorer who lived in Louisville and Clarksville and died in 1791. Only a few of the papers in the series are those of the explorer William Clark and they deal with Indian affairs from 1814 to 1822. These seem out of place with the other papers in the series. It might be the case that those few younger William Clark items were filed with his cousin's by accident, perhaps because the name was the same. Perhaps the explorer left those Indian papers in Louisville with family while there for a visit and never retrieved them. If that is the case, then Draper might have gotten the elder William Clark's papers from a Louisville Clark or Croghan. If Draper got the papers from descendants of the younger William Clark (he was in contact with at least three of Clark's sons—Meriwether Lewis Clark, George Rogers Hancock Clark, and Jefferson Kearny Clark) as believed, then William might have gotten the elder William's papers due to his Clarksville land interests to which many of the papers relate.

A possible clue to this line of possession might be the early George Rogers Clark and some cousin William Clark papers acquired by the Missouri Historical Society in the 1920s from Julia Clark

Voorhis, a granddaughter of William Clark. The series are arranged thusly: J—George Rogers Clark Papers; K—George Rogers Clark Miscellanies; L—Jonathan Clark Papers; M—William Clark Papers; N—William Croghan Papers. Since Series L is believed to have come from Jonathan's son Isaac and Series N from John Croghan, it would seem that one of these sources might have had Floyd's journal until acquired by Draper. It is also possible that some of the Clark papers, and the Floyd journal, came from one of William Clark's descendants, if those papers in Series M are viewed as possibly coming from the same group of papers that later made their way to Missouri Historical. This reasoning could also all be for naught. Harry Miller of the Wisconsin Historical Society has warned me that Draper did not maintain collections by their provenance, and their order should not be taken as an indication of their source. Josephine Harper also states this in her guide to the Draper collection. It could be the case that when placement of the journal was decided, it was simply placed with William Clark material due to the expedition link of the two men—its origin in the collection unknown. It would seem, however, that a Clark source is most likely. See Harper, *Guide to the Draper Manuscripts,* pp. xxi–xxii, 67–73; Moulton, 2:538; author's personal communication with Harry Miller, February 2004.

40. *The Nation,* p. 471; Coues, *In Memoriam,* pp. 21–22. George Perkins was a board member and officer of the Floyd Memorial Association and editor and publisher of the *Sioux City Journal.* It is easily understood why such extensive coverage was given the Association and its activities in the pages of that paper. He was also the area's representative in Congress from 1891 to 1899 and helped secure funding for the monument.

41. Coues, *In Memoriam,* pp. 22–24.

42. Coues, *In Memoriam,* pp. 23–24; *Sioux City Journal,* 21 August 1895, p. 5; *Sioux City Sunday Journal,* section 3, 26 November 1950, p. 1.

43. Coues, *In Memoriam,* pp. 24–32.

44. Coues, *In Memoriam,* pp. 26–27; *Sioux City Journal,* 21 August 1895, p. 1.

45. Coues, *In Memoriam,* pp. 27–29. P. C. Waltermire was paid $15 for his services in 1895 (Floyd Memorial Association, pp. 95–96). He does not appear again in the financial accounts regarding the 1900 and 1901 ceremonies because he was hired by the *Sioux City Journal* to take photographs. Perkins apparently included the expense as part of the *Journal's* coverage of the Floyd monument project. No complete set of monument related photographs for this time period have been located as of yet. When the *Journal* changed ownership in the early 1970s, many of the old records were discarded. Assuming that the newspaper must have had a set of Waltermire's photographs of the monument project, it is possible that they were included in this house cleaning. A query to the Iowa Historical Society met with no success regarding such photographs in its collection. It is possible that papers of some of the prominent individuals involved might contain them, and if extant they may be found under those titles. Therefore, at this time, the photographs in the collections of The Filson Historical Society and the Sioux City Public Museum (SCPM) are the only known views of the 1895, 1900, and 1901 activities concerning the Floyd reburial and monument. The Filson has ten photographs regarding the Floyd grave site and monument, and the SCPM nine. Some of the views are duplicates, but there are eleven different views between them. The *Journal* published six photos (three of which the SCPM does not have, but The Filson does) in its 1950 article. In addition, notes on the back of some of the photos in the SCPM collection (and not in the 1950 article) indicate they have been published. If they were published the publication has not been identified. It seems likely that views other than those at The Filson and the SCPM were taken. The records of the ceremonies refer to at least one view taken for which neither institution has a photo.

46. Coues, *In Memoriam,* pp. 29–53; *Sioux City Journal,* 21 August 1895, pp. 1–2, 5. A second urn was acquired because upon preparing the grave site and remaining bones for the ceremony, it was discovered that the one intended to hold all the bones was not tall enough for the leg bones. The remains reburied were: the skull with lower jaw; right femur, 18 inches long; a tibia, 15 inches long; a fibula, 14.75 inches long; part of the other fibula; one vertebra; one clavicle; and portions of several ribs. The inscription on the urn made by Holman Brothers specially for the remains read: "Sgt Charles Floyd/Died Aug 20th 1804./Reinterred May 28, 1857./Memorial Services August 20, 1895." The marble slab, made by M. C. Carlstrom, was inscribed: "Sergeant/CHARLES FLOYD/DIED/Aug. 20. 1804./Remains removed from 600/Feet West and Reburied at/This Place May 28. 1857./This Stone Placed/Aug. 20. 1895." The 1901 report of the Association only mentions discussion about a suitable disposition of the slab. No mention is made of what was done with it. Iowa Historical does not have the marble marker or cast of Floyd's skull in its collection.

It seems rather shocking today that the original Floyd journal was placed at risk by allowing Butler to take it to Sioux City; but at that time the attitudes regarding this kind of material were different and exceptions were made and such actions allowed. Coues was permitted by the American Philosophical Society to remove the original Lewis and Clark journals from its library and take them to his home in Washington, D.C., while he worked on his history of the expedition. Thwaites was allowed access to them at his home in Madison. Butler was allowed to carry Floyd's journal to the monument dedication in 1901 also.

47. Coues, *In Memoriam,* pp. 55–56. The records state four grandsons, but actually it was three grandsons and one son. They were his son, Jefferson Kearney Clark (1824–1900), of St. Louis, and grandsons Col. William Hancock Clark (1839–1922), of Detroit, Col. Meriwether Lewis Clark Jr. (1846–1899), of Louisville, and Maj. John O'Fallon Clark (1844–1916), of St. Louis. William and M. Lewis were sons of

Meriwether Lewis Clark, and John of George Rogers
Hancock Clark. By 1899 only William H. Clark
was still on the board and he does not appear after
that year.

48. Floyd Memorial Association, pp. 13–16.

49. Floyd Memorial Association, pp. 13–16, 20–22.
George Perkins, as a member of the House of Representatives from Iowa's Eleventh District (which
included Sioux City), introduced H.R. 11181, "An
Act to Provide for the Erection of a Monument to
Sergeant Charles Floyd," on 15 December 1898 in
the 3rd Session of the 55th Congress. The legislation
requested $10,000 in funding support for the monu-
ment. The proposal apparently elicited no debate. It
was referred to the Committee on the Library, which
reported it without amendment, accompanied by
report number 2022, to the Committee on the Whole
House. Incorporating information received from the
Floyd Memorial Association, the report noted that
the project was a "fitting monument commemorative
of that expedition and of the first soldier in the service
of the United States to lay down his life within the
Louisiana Purchase." The session was in its closing
days by this time, and Perkins determined that no
action on the bill would occur. To secure some level
of immediate funding, he and U.S. senator William
Allison of Iowa successfully secured a monument
funding amendment to the general deficiency bill
for a $5,000 appropriation.

50. Floyd Memorial Association, pp. 16–18, 22–23,
30–36; Chittenden, pp. 3827–33. The original re-
quest to the Iowa legislature was $10,000, but like
the federal appropriation, the amount was reduced
to $5,000. Hiram M. Chittenden had replaced
Sanford as superintendent of the Sioux City Corps
office in October 1899. Like the Coues and Floyd
Memorial Association reports, Chittenden's 1901
annual (and final) report on the erection of the
Floyd monument is an excellent and authoritative
source.

51. Floyd Memorial Association, pp. 36–38; Chittenden,
p. 3831. The proportion of the concrete was: 1 part
"Atlas" cement, 2.37 parts bank sand from Waterbury,
Neb., and 4.37 parts crushed rock from the Sioux
Falls granite quarries. Eleven huge vats of water were
used in mixing the materials into concrete. The *Journal* differed slightly regarding a few specifics. It put
the work at lasting ten hours and thirty-five minutes,
instead of Chittenden's nine hours and fifty minutes,
and 143 cubic yards of concrete being used rather
than 138.6. Because Chittenden was the director of
the project, I have generally used his data. At this time

it had not yet been decided whether to exhume the
sergeant's remains yet again and deposit them in the
monument.

52. Floyd Memorial Association, pp. 38–46; Chittenden,
pp. 3831–32. The *Journal* reports one urn being
used, but two had been used in 1895. It is possible
that another urn was made for the occasion, but it is
more likely that both the 1895 urns were deposited
in the monument. The copper box "time capsule"
contained documents and printed works concerning
the monument, the Association, the Lewis and Clark
Expedition, Iowa laws, Sioux City, as well as newspapers, U.S. coins and postage stamps, a GAR button,
and a photograph of Association president Charles.
The ceremony ended at 3:15. The cornerstone was
laid at the northeast corner of the monument. On
the north side was inscribed: "August 20, A.D. 1900,
Madison B. Davis, Commander, Department of Iowa,
Grand Army of the Republic; and on the east side
H. M. Chittenden, Captain, Corps of Engineers,
U.S.A., Engineer and Architect."

53. Floyd Memorial Association, pp. 49–51, 66–67;
Chittenden, pp. 3832. Hansen Brothers of Sioux
City had been awarded the contract for erecting the
monument and doing the paving around the base.
Hermann & Savage of Sioux City received the contract for the steel fence that was to surround the
monument. The two bronze tablets to be set in the
monument were manufactured by the Gorham
Manufacturing Company of New York. One tablet
was for Floyd and the shaft, and the other com-
memorated the Louisiana Purchase and the Lewis
and Clark Expedition.

54. Chittenden, pp. 687, 3829–30, 3832–33. The steel
fence was seven-and-a-half feet high. The vertical
bars were one-inch square, bent outward at the top
and sharpened.

55. Floyd Memorial Association, pp. 55–81; *Sioux City
Journal,* 30 May 1901, pp. 1, 6–7, and 31 May 1901,
pp. 1, 6–7. Coues had died on Christmas Day 1899.
John A. Kasson was an Iowan who had served as a
diplomat and U.S. congressman and was a nationally
known orator. Speeches of this length were quite
usual and would have been expected from a noted
speaker on such an occasion.

56. Floyd Memorial Association, pp. 81–85; *Sioux
City Journal,* 31 May 1901, p. 6.

57. Chittenden, p. 3833.

58. Floyd Memorial Association, p. 93. This poem
appeared in the 30 May 1901 edition of the *Sioux
City Tribune,* together with an editorial regarding
the monument.

The Journal of Sergeant Charles Floyd
14 May–18 August 1804

THE JOURNALS OF WILLIAM CLARK, JOHN ORDWAY, JOSEPH WHITE-house, Patrick Gass, and Charles Floyd chronicle their experiences—the adventure, hardship, danger, work, and wonder of discovery. Meriwether Lewis kept no known journal for the journey upriver to the Mandan-Hidatsa villages where the Corps' winter encampment, Fort Mandan, was established. Robert Frazer kept a journal, but it has never been found. Nathaniel H. Pryor probably kept one—the sergeants were ordered to by Lewis and Clark, and Clark makes reference to his "papers"—but if he did, it also is lost. A couple of other men might have kept journals, but if they did, they too have been lost to history.

Floyd never reached the villages of the Arikaras or the camp of the Shoshones. He succumbed to illness before the wonders the expedition experienced really began to be encountered. His journal is the briefest of the surviving accounts but it, unlike some of the others, has survived. His faithful daily entries until two days before his death provide an important record of the expedition. Floyd never complained. He does not mention the misery caused by mosquitoes, heat, and other hardships. He makes no mention of his own activities for the most part but does on occasion note those of others. Floyd provides no accounts of close calls on a river that was beautiful but also dangerous. He does not even mention being sick until after Clark noted it.

The young explorer's journal is a simple, straightforward account of the basic occurrences of the journey—a day-to-day struggle to ascend the wild, unpredictable, and dangerous Missouri. It is written with great brevity. Where they camped, the distance traveled, the coming and going of hunters and their success, travelers encountered coming downstream, and a description of the land—especially a description of the land—was what Floyd regularly recorded. He seems to be appraising the country and its appeal to the American settlers—in his mind, perhaps even his own family—that would follow in the wake of Lewis and Clark. Labored over at the end of a long and tiring day, the reader can imagine the young sergeant with journal on knee, in the light of the campfire, diligently recording the major events of the day's journey and the progress they had made. Often not more than a few lines, Floyd faithfully carried out his captains' orders to record "all passing occurences, and such other observations on the country &c. as shall appear to them worthy of notice." Perhaps he would have become more descriptive in time. While keeping the sparsest entries of the surviving journals, Floyd was capable of noting an interesting event or recording an informative observation. His premature death and the end of his journal are a true loss to knowing more about this American epic.

The physical journal itself is nondescript. Floyd kept his journal in a common bound book of blank paper covered with marbled boards. Floyd turned the book so that the spine is at the top and the journal opens and is read vertically, just as Lewis and Clark did with the books used for their fair copy journals. Oriented this way, each page measures 7½ inches wide by 5⅞ inches long. The journal itself consists of fifty-three written pages, plus one page of notes, as well as notes on the inside of each of the covers, thus totaling fifty-six pages. In addition, there are the stubs of three sheets, two of which have writing on them, that were cut out of the journal by an unknown person at an unknown date. Floyd was literate but his handwriting appears somewhat labored and deliberate. His spelling and grammar indicate a limited education. The young explorer read what he wrote and made revisions as he deemed necessary. Edits were made using strikethroughs, smeared inkblots, and insertions. Others read what he wrote also, as evidenced by William Clark's additions and the obvious sharing of information among the journal keepers.

The provenance of the journal is uncertain. In the past it has been theorized that the journal was sent back down the Missouri in the spring of 1805 with the keelboat and subsequently delivered to Floyd's family. At an unknown date, Lyman Draper acquired it for his collection, possibly from a Floyd family member, and it subsequently disappeared into Draper's vast collection of manuscripts that he left to the Wisconsin Historical Society. There it lay unknown and forgotten until 1893, when Reuben Gold Thwaites of the Society found it. Although Floyd's journal definitely ended up in Draper's collection, its passage from the deceased sergeant to the voracious collector might have followed a different trail. Lewis stated in April 1805 from Fort Mandan that one of the sergeant's journals was being sent to his agent in St. Louis to try to assure its survival. Was this Floyd's journal? Since he was dead and the other sergeants were still keeping their journals, it would seem most likely that it was. No mention is made of returning it to Floyd's family. If Lewis kept it until his death in 1809 and it then devolved to Clark, perhaps the latter retained possession of it. If so, it either remained in his family or perhaps passed to the family of his brother Jonathan Clark or sister Lucy Croghan. Draper acquired manuscripts in the mid-nineteenth century from both those families and it is also believed from descendants of William Clark. No known manuscripts were acquired from the Floyd family. Draper kept no records of his acquisitions, so the exact path that the Floyd journal traveled to the collector remains a mystery.

Once the journal was discovered among Draper's collection, it quickly received national attention. Professor James D. Butler of Madison and a member of the American Antiquarian Society presented a paper on the journal to that society in 1894. Both Butler's paper and the journal were published by the Society that same year. It served as an inspiration to those working to preserve the remains of the sergeant and to build a monument in his honor. In 1905, Thwaites published it in volume seven of his edition of the Lewis and Clark journals.

The most recent publication of the journal is in editor Gary E. Moulton's definitive edition of the expedition journals published by the University of Nebraska Press. Moulton's masterful edition of the journals, including the annotations, allows an unparalleled comparison of the extant journals of the explorers and enables the reader to gain a true understanding of and appreciation for the Corps' experience. His edition was the single-most important source in editing and annotating this edition of the Floyd journal.

The original journal of Sergeant Charles Floyd resides in the Draper Manuscripts at the Wisconsin Historical Society. Some people will have had the opportunity to view the original journal as part of Lewis and Clark exhibits. For those who have not seen the journal, and also for those who have, enjoy seeing *every* page in this facsimile edition of the journal of a young man who went exploring with Lewis and Clark.

A Journal Commenced at River Dubois — monday 14 th 180

may 14 th 1804 Showery day Capt Clark Set out at

3 oclock P m for the western expidition the party

Consisted of 3 Serguntee and 38 working hands which maned

the Battow and two Perogues we Sailed up the meſsouria

6 miles and encamped on the N. side of the River

Tuesday may 15 th 1804 Rainey morniy fair wind the

later part of the day Sailed 9om and encamped on

the N. side some Land Cleared the Soil verry Rich —

Wedensday may 16 th 1804 Set out eriley this moring plesent

arrived at St Charles at 2 oclock. P m one Gung Fired

a Grait nomber of Friench peaple Came to see the Boat

&c. this place is an old Friench village & Roman

A Journal commenced at River Dubois — Monday
~~14th 180~~ may 14ᵗʰ 1804 Showery day Capt Clark Set
out at 3 oclock P m for the western expidition the party
Consisted of 3 Serguntes and 38 working hands which
maned the Batteow and two Perogues¹ we Sailed up the
missouria 6 miles and encamped on the N. Side of the
River Tusday may 15ᵗʰ 1804 Rainey mornig fair wind
the Later part of the day Sailed Som and encamped on
the N. Side Some Land Cleared the Soil verry Rich —
Wend̶day may 16ᵗʰ 1804 Set out eriley this moring
plesent arrived at Sᵗ Charles at 2 oclock P m one Gune
Fired a Grait nomber of Friench people Came to See
the Boat &c this place is an old French village & Roman

1. All the extant enlisted men's journals state
that three sergeants and thirty-eight working
hands departed Camp Dubois (or Camp River
a Dubois). They may well have compared notes
on this. If so, it is an immediate example of the
men conferring and borrowing from each other
regarding their journal keeping. This group
sometimes included William Clark, as evidenced
in Charles Floyd's journal. While Clark, and
later Meriwether Lewis when he kept a journal,
might have consulted the enlisted men's journals, it is most likely that the latter consulted
their captains' writings. Apparently, 14 May
wasn't a day Clark and the men shared information. Clark's number for the men leaving
their winter camp on this date varies from that
of the men. These numbers would change at
St. Charles and the composition of the boats
and squads/messes would change on 26 May
when new detachment orders were issued. At
that time the entire party included forty-five
men. The craft were the keelboat (or *bateaux*,
as it was also called) and two pirogues known
as the red and white pirogues. The red one was
the larger of the two and manned by the French
boatmen. It was also sometimes called the
"French" boat or pirogue. The white one was
manned by the soldiers temporarily attached
to the expedition until sent back in the spring of
1805 with the keelboat. In addition to the indivi-
dual journals of the expedition edited by Gary E.
Moulton, the one-volume abridged edition, also
edited by Moulton, offers selections from all the
journals for each day. (Moulton, *Journals of the
Lewis and Clark Expedition*, 2:228–29, 254–56,
509–29.) Note: All Moulton citations hereafter
refer to this multivolume work.

Cattolick Some american setled in the Country
Countrey around F. Thursday may 17th 1804
a fair day but Rainey night Friday may 18th 1804
we lay at St Charles Saturday may 19th 1804
a Rainey day Capt Lewis Joined us
Sunday may 20th 1804 ~~nothing worth Relating~~ the day
~~party went to~~ ~~~~
~~we 8.c~~ monday 21th 1804 Left St Charles at
4 oclk. Pm ~~~~ Showery encamped on the N Side
of the River Tuesday may 22 1804 Set out
after a very hard Rain and passed Bonnin
Creek on th South Side of the River Came 15 mi

encamped on the Nd Side of the River at Cliftes
Some Indianes Came to see us wensday may the 23
1804 we Set out at 6 oclock A.m. plesent passed day
the wife of osogs River ~~three~~ miles and half we
pased the tavern or Cave anoled place on the
South Side of the River 120 Long 20 feet in
Debth 40 feet purpendickler on the South
Side of the River high Cliftes one mile to a ~~crle~~
Creek Called tavern Creek and encamped on
the South Side of the River our armes and
amunition Inspicted Thursday may 24th 1804
nothen Remarkble ~~a we~~ nothing ocord this
day Encamped on South Side

Catholeck   Some american Setled in the ~~Contry~~ Countrey
around.[2] ~~T~~ Thursday may 17th 1804   a fair but Rainey
Night   Friday may 18th 1804   we Lay at S[t] Charles   Satur-
day may 19th 1804   a Rainey day   Capt Lewis Joined us — [3]
Sunday may 20th 1804   ~~and   a number of the party went to~~
~~the mass and Saw them perform and~~ &c.   [^]nothing worth
Relating to day[^] &c.   monday 21th 1804   Left S[t] Charles
at 4 oclk. P m   Showerey   encamped on the N Side of the
River   Tusday may 22nd 1804   Set out after a verry hard
Rain and passed Bonnon Creek on the South Side of the
River   came 15 mi[les]

encamped on the N. Side of the River at cliftes   Some
Indianes Came to See us   wensday may the 23d 1804   we
Set out at 6 oclock Am   plesent day passed the wife of
osogs ~~R~~ River three miles and half   we pased the tavern
or Cave a noted place on the South Side of the River
120 Long 20 feet in Debth 40 feet purpendickler on the
South Side of the River   high Cliftes one mile to a ~~cre~~
Creek Colled Tavern Creek and encamped on the South
Side of the River   our armes and amunition Inspected[4]
Thursday may 24th 1804   nothin Remarkble ~~as we~~
Nothing acord this day   encamped ~~of~~ on South Side[5]

2. There were about 450 inhabitants in 1803
   St. Charles, primarily Roman Catholic French.
   Americans were increasingly settling the
   countryside around the town. Clark, Lewis,
   and Joseph Whitehouse all provide good
   descriptions of the town and its residents
   at the time of the Corps of Discovery's visit.
   (Moulton, 2:232–33, 234 n, 241–42; 11:9.)
3. Floyd, John Ordway, and Whitehouse report
   that Lewis arrived in St. Charles on 19 May.
   Patrick Gass's edited journal does not give
   an exact date. Lewis and Clark, however, report that he arrived on 20 May and that is the
   accepted date. Why the enlisted men were off
   one day is not known. Perhaps it is an early
   example of them borrowing from each other
   and thus sometimes perpetuating erroneous
   information. Lewis provides a good description
   of his trip from St. Louis, where he had been
   delayed in making some final preparations, to
   St. Charles. It is one of his few known journal-
   type entries for that first year up the Missouri.
   (Moulton, 2:240–43.)
4. It was an eventful day on 23 May. Floyd's
   "wife of osogs River" is Clark's Osage Woman
   or Femme Osage River. It still bears the latter
   name today. This is an example of names of
   watercourses sometimes differing slightly in
   name—and occasionally completely in name—
   among the journal keepers. Overall, they are
   generally consistent and their sharing of information was effective. The Corps almost
   suffered a disaster and likely end to the expedition when Lewis nearly fell from Tavern Rock
   while investigating the bluff and cave. None of
   the enlisted men comment on Lewis's mishap,
   perhaps believing it inappropriate or against
   military propriety or orders to report something like this concerning an officer and their
   commander. Perhaps trying to make sure he
   observed and noted military procedure, Floyd
   generally notes any inspections by the captains,
   as he did on this date. Sometimes that simple
   notation indicates a more important occurrence,
   such as a court martial, which he did note. The
   Corps also passed Boone's Settlement, a group
   of Americans composed in part of family members and associates of famous Kentucky frontiersman Daniel Boone, who had settled there
   in 1799. The explorers apparently did not meet
   Boone. (Moulton, 2:245–49.)
5. Floyd's entry for 24 May is a model of understatement. He, Ordway, and Whitehouse make
   no reference to the keelboat getting turned in
   the current after the towrope broke and being
   in danger of turning over. Clark described the
   event in some detail, and Gass mentioned it.
   (Moulton, 2:249–51; 10:9.)

Friday may 25th 1804 Set out and came 4
miles passed a creek called Wood River on the
south Side the Land is good & handsom the Soil
Rich & high Banks encamped at a French
village called St Johns This is the Last
Setelment of whites on this River ——

Saturday may 26th 1804 we Set out at
7 OClock A m 2 of our men was Sent with the Horses by Land to meat us that night hard thunder and Rain
this morning passed a creek called otter
Creek encamped on the N. Side

Sunday may 27th 1804 passed ash creek ——
— on the South Side high clifts on S Side
arrived at the mouth of the Gasgarade River
at 5 ock P m on the South Side encamped
on an Island oppeset the mouth of the River
which is a handsom Situation high hiles on the
Left Side the Bottom is of good quallity &c
armes and ammunitian Inspected ——

monday may 28th 1804 rain Last night
Severall men went hunting &c
one of them killed a Deer Tuesday may 29th
1804 Rain Last night Set out at 5 ock P m
came 3 miles encamped
&c Came 3 miles passed Deer Creek
on the S. Side encamped all night

Friday may 25ᵗʰ 1804 Set out and Came 4 miles passed
a Creek Colled wood River on the South ˄Side₍˄₎ the
Land is Good & hundsom the Soil Rich & high Banks
encamped at a French village Colled Sᵗ Johns this is
the Last Setelment of whites on this River — ⁶ Saturday
may 26ᵗʰ 1804 we Set out at 7 oclock A m ₍˄₎2 of our men
was Sent with the Horses by Land to meat us that night⁷
but₍˄₎ hard thunder and Rain this morning passed a creek
Colled otter Creek encamped on the N. Side Sunday
may 27ᵗʰ 1804 pased ash Creek —

on the South Side high Clifts on S Side arrived at the
mouthe of the Gasganade River at 5 ock P.m on the South
Side encamped on an Island oppeset the mouth of the
River which is a handsom Situation high hiles on the
Left Side the Bottom is of Good quallity &c. armes
and ammunition Inspected — ⁸
monday may 28ᵗʰ 1804 rain Last night Severall men
went ~~hun~~ owt hunting &c. one of them Killed a Deer
Tuesday may 29ᵗʰ 1804 Rain Last night Set out at
5 ock P m ~~[c]ame 3 miles encamped 5 o~~ Came 3 miles
pssded Deer Creek on the S. Side encamped all Night

6. The small settlement was also called by the
French name La Charette. The name St. John's
came from the Spanish fort San Juan del Misuri
established there in 1796. French and Americans lived there by 1800. Boone later moved
to the area and died there. The original town
site was washed away by the Missouri River.
Marthasville is the closest present town. Expedition veteran John Colter settled in the vicinity,
on the south side of the Missouri, in 1810 after
returning from the West and his many adventures and close calls. (Moulton, 2:251–53.)

7. Floyd routinely recorded the coming and going
of the hunters, so important to providing the
meat to feed the men and their voracious appe-
tites due to the hard physical work they did
on a daily basis. The two hunters mentioned
here are George Drouillard and John Shields.
Next to the captains, Drouillard was the most
indispensable member of the expedition, serving as hunter, interpreter, and scout (also see
note 13). Shields was also one of the party's
best hunters in addition to his duties as the primary gunsmith and blacksmith. Floyd might
have known Shields before the expedition since
they both joined at the Falls of the Ohio. Clark
stated in his journal that the two men were instructed to travel one day upriver and then hunt
the next. This apparently indicates that they
could make by land in one day what it took
the keelboat two days to travel. Drouillard
and Shields did not actually rejoin the party
until 2 June—a little worse for the wear but
impressed with the country they had passed
through. Floyd generally does not name the
hunters sent out, and they will not regularly
be identified in these notes. However, the primary hunters were Drouillard and the Nine
Young Men from Kentucky (excepting Sgts.
Floyd and Pryor). Floyd and the other enlisted
journal keepers make no mention of the detachment orders issued that day setting forth
the duties of the sergeants and the revised
squad and mess arrangements. (Moulton,
2:54, 269–70, 516; 10:11.)

8. Floyd rarely neglected to note an inspection,
as already mentioned. Because 27 May was
the first day of travel under the new detachment orders, the captains might have called the
inspection to see how they were being carried
out and working. Ordway also noted an inspection for that day, but Clark recorded one on
28 May. If there were two inspections or an
error regarding the date by one or two of the
journalists, it is unknown.

Just above on the South Side on man Lost hunting
French men Left for him ~~Wensday may~~

~~20th 1804~~ ~~wednsday set out after a verry~~
~~hard rain Last night Raind all the with~~
~~thunder and hail~~

Wedsday 30th 1804 Set out 7 OClk after a verry
hard Rain and thunder it Rained During the
greatest part of the day with hail passed one
Creek ~~Called~~ on the South Side Colled Rush Creek the
Land is Low. Bottom but Rich Soil 3 miles to River on
the N Side Colled Littel muddy River the Land
is Some what Like the Laer it comes in opsett
an Isld 2 miles to River on the South Side Colled
painter River it Comes in opsett to Isd in the midst
                    South Side
of the milssoura encamped at the mouth

Thursday may 31th 1804 one peroque Loaded with
Barke Skins and Beaver and deer Skins from the ~~osages~~
village one ~~osages~~ woman with them our hunters wen
out and kild one Deer we Lay By all this day on
acount of the wind the Land is good but Broken
it Rained and Cleard up ~~nothing~~ worth Relating to day

Sunday
June 1 1804 Set out come one mile past one River
on the N Side colled Big mudy River comes in opsett
the Lower pint of willow Island the Land is of good
quallity as any I ever Saw but Low 4 two miles so bear Creek
on the South Side High Hill on the Laer Side it is about 30
~~Several Indians~~ Came 11 miles ~~encamped at the mouth of~~
~~the Gra osage River the wind from the west~~
~~theday~~

Jest above on the South Side on[e] man Lost hunting
French men Left for him⁹   wensday may ~~30ᵗʰ 1804~~
~~wedneday Set out after a verry har rain Last night~~
~~Rained all this with thunder and hail~~

wedsday 30ᵗʰ 1804 Set out 7 ock after a verry hard Rain
and Thunder it Rained During the Gratiest part of the
day with hail passed one Creek ~~Colled Rush~~ ₍^₎on₍^₎ the
South Side colled Rush Creek the Land is Low Bottom
but Rich Soil 3 miles to River on the N Side Colled Littel
muddy River the Land is Some what Like the Loer, it
comes in opset ~~th~~ an ISˡᵈ 2 miles to River on the South Side
Colled painter River it Comes in opset to ISᵈ in the midel

of the missoura encamped ₍ₐ₎South Side₍^₎ ¹⁰ at the mouth —
thursday may 31ᵗʰ 1804 one perogue Loaded with Bare
Skins and Beaver and Deer Skins from the osogs~~es~~
village¹¹ one osog~~es~~ woman with them our hunters went
out and Kild one Deer we Lay By all this day on acount
of the wind the Land is Good but Broken it Rained and
Cleard up nothing worth Relating to day ₍^₎Friday₍^₎
June 1ᵗ 1804 Set out come one mile past one River on
the N Side colled Big mudy River comes in opset the
Louer pint [point] of willow Island the Land is of Good
quallity as aney I ever Saw but Low two miles to Bear
Creek on the South Side High Hill on the Loer Side it is
about 30 — yardes in weth [width] at the mouth of ~~water~~
~~verry Strong past Several Isˡᵈ Came 12 miles encamped~~
~~at the mouth of the Gran osoge River the wind from the~~
~~west the day Clear~~

9. The man was Whitehouse. According to
   Whitehouse, he was not lost. He related that
   on 28 May he had found and explored a cave
   while hunting. Upon returning to the river, he
   discovered that the keelboat and white pirogue
   had both moved on and the red, or "French,"
   pirogue had been left behind to wait for him.
   The other journalists state that this occurred
   on 29 May. It appears likely that Whitehouse
   got confused on his days and "lost" one. Clark
   and Ordway noted hearing gunfire that evening
   and assuming it was the French boatmen firing
   their guns as signals to help Whitehouse find
   them. Whitehouse makes no mention of this,
   however. He relates that he easily met up with
   the red pirogue upon returning to the river, that
   they could not catch up that night to the main
   party, but did overtake them on the evening
   of 29 [most likely 30] May. Floyd and Ordway
   make no mention of when the red pirogue
   rejoined the party. Gass (or his editor David
   McKeehan) incorrectly stated that Whitehouse
   did not rejoin them until 1 June. Unless Whitehouse did some journal copying when he
   reunited with his comrades, he is clearly back
   with the main party on 30 May. (Moulton,
   2:261, 264; 9:8; 10:10–11; 11:14–15.)

10. Although "South Side" is written at the bottom
    of the previous page, Floyd clearly intended
    for it to be inserted in the sentence at the top
    of the page. Because Floyd had room above the
    sentence to write the words, he apparently was
    not bothered to write it on what we think of as
    the previous page, since orienting the journal
    vertically placed the binding in the middle of
    what Floyd probably considered one page.

11. The Corps did not meet either the Great Osage
    or the Little Osage. Clark's entry for the day
    states that the pirogue was a *cajeu*, a French-
    Canadian term for a small raft made by lashing
    together two canoes. Two men and one woman
    comprised the party and had come from the
    Great Osage villages on the Arkansas River in
    Kansas. Another group of Great Osage and their
    kinsmen the Little Osage lived on the Osage
    River in western Missouri. (Moulton, 2:260 n,
    266–67.)

the day ~~Clear~~ Clear wind from the west water strong
at Came 12 miles past several 93 d$ encamped at ~~Boelts~~
~~as~~ the mouth of the
Grand osage River Saterday June 2d 1804 Lay Bey all this
day for observations 4 men went out hunting Killd H Deer
the day war Clear wind from the South the Land is of a
Good Quallity High hiles on the S side a good Lick on the
South S side it is a bout one mill and half from
the mouth of the Gran osage Dow the River
in the a Butifull punt Between the two Rivers hills
putts in a bout a mile Betwen thes two the
second Bank it high at the mouthe of this River
~~in the~~ punt a Butifull N C Best Below the River
it Lays in the midel of the Rivers our hunters Retun
haw had Ben with our horses 8 day and say the Country
is as good as aney thay Ever Saw armes inspected all

in good order
~~Friday ~~ 1804 ~~Sunday June 3d 1804~~

The missorea 4875 yardes wide osage River 397 —
yardes wider we fell a number of trell at the punt
for the porpal of obeservations

Sunday June 3d 1804 Set out at 4 oclock P m
the fore part of the day Clear the latter part
and Rain wind from E S
Clou day with Thunder Capt Lewis and J. Druvery
went hunting Kild one Deer & Grown hog 4 miles
to River murrow on the South Saide it is
a bout 30 yardes wide and High Cliffes on the Loer
Side of it & thundered yardes up the River Cliffes
encamped at the mouth on the South Side our
hunters Kild one Deer Monday June 4th
Set out the Clear morning 5 miles By our Stersman
Let the Boat Run under a lim and Broke ~~it~~

the day Claer [^]Clear[^] wind from the west water Strong
Came 12 miles   past Several I^Slds encamped at the 4 oclk
at the mouth of the Grann osoge River   Saterday June 2^d
1804   Lay By all this day for observations 4 men went out
hunting Killed 4 Deer the day was Clear wind from the
South the Land is of a Good quallity High hiles on the
S. Side a good Lick on the South S. Side it is about one
mile and half from the mouth of the Gran osoge Dow[n]
the River a Butifull p[o]int Betwen the two Rivers hills
in [^]the[^] pnts in about a mile Betwen the two the Second
Bank is high at the mouthe of this Riv [^]River[^] River at
[^]in the[^] pint a Butifull Is^d Jest Below the pint it Lays
in the midel of the Rivers our hunters Return how [who]
had Ben with our horses 8 day and Say the cuntry is as
good as aney thay ever Saw armes inspected all

Sunday June 3^d 1804   Sunday June 3rd 1804 [^]in Good
order[^] the missorea is 875 yardes wide osage River
397 — yardes widee we fell a nomber of trees at the pint
for the porpas of oberservations[12]

Sunday June 3^d 1804 Set out at 4 o clock P. m the for part
of the day Clear the Latter part Clouday with thunder
[^]and Rain wind from ES^t[^] Capt Lewis and G. Druruy[13]
went hunting   Kild one Deer & Grown [ground] hog
4 miles to River murrow on the South Saide Hit is about
30 yardes wide and High Cliftes on the Loer Side of it
3 hundrered yardes up the River Cliftes encamped at the
mouth on the South Side ouer hunters Kild one Deer
Smonday 4th June 4th Set out the Clear morning 2 miles
By ouer Stersman[14] Let the Boat Run under a lim and
Broke off

12. All the journal keepers noted to varying degrees
the captains' efforts to take astronomical readings, Whitehouse and Ordway more so than
Floyd and Gass (per his published journal). This
is one record that Lewis is known to have kept
during this leg of the trip (Codex O of the journals). Putting the men to felling trees to better
take the readings indicates their efforts to get
good, accurate readings. (Moulton, 2:269–74.)

13. This is the first mention of Drouillard by name
in Floyd's journal. He was of French Canadian–
Shawnee parentage and had been raised on the
frontier. He had joined at Fort Massac on the
lower Ohio River and was promptly sent to Tennessee to locate the detachment of soldiers that
had failed to rendezvous with the party at Massac.
He rejoined the Corps at Camp Dubois with the
detachment and officially joined the Corps on
25 December 1803—a wonderful Christmas
present for the captains. He is among the most
frequently mentioned men in the journals and
apparently was held in great regard and even
admiration by the party's members. A thorough
reading of the journals indicates that those keeping journals, and therefore almost certainly the
other men as well, clearly believed that this
French Canadian–Shawnee hunter, woodsman,
and interpreter possessed abilities beyond theirs.
The captains clearly relied on him heavily and
regarded him highly. He returned to the West
after the expedition and was killed by Blackfeet
in 1810 near the Three Forks of the Missouri. A
biography of Drouillard was published in 1964.
A growing list of articles has also been written
about this talented frontiersman and explorer,
as well as a historical novel. (Moulton, 2:516;
Holmberg, 67; Holmberg, "A Man of Much
Merit: George Drouillard," pp. 8–12; Holmberg, "Getting out the Word," pp. 15, 17 n;
Skarsten; Thom.)

14. The steersman was Ordway. Clark says only
that the sergeant at the helm was responsible.
Ordway identifies himself as that sergeant,
writing that he steered the boat too close to
the shore and the mast's stay got caught in a
sycamore limb with the result that the mast
broke very easily. This accident also provides
evidence of the days the sergeants might have
been manning their assigned posts in the keelboat if the three-day rotation as stated in the
26 May detachment orders had not been devi-
ated from. (Moulton, 2:275; 9:9–10.)

our mast off 3 miles past a Creek no the South
~~side Colled mast Creek on the~~
~~no more fit to bote Colet~~ Rich Land Creek a
a Butifull apear of Land as ever I have walnut Shoger tree
ash and mulber trees Level on both Sides land this Creek is Clear
watter about 30 yardes wide one mile past a River on
the N. Side Colled ~~Cedar~~ River the Land is Level and good
4 miles past Creek Colled ~~Jon Cer~~ Creek on the S Side
at the Loer pint of Is.d on the same 3 miles to a pint
on the N.d Colled Batere De charma prarie on the S Sid
high Cliftes on the South Strong water came 10 miles
over hunters kild 8 Deer encaint on the
South Side under the Cliftes set out Tuesday June 5t
fair day passed Lead Creek on South Side of the River
Littel good woman Creek on the N. Side came
9 miles past the Creek of the Big Rock 15 ya⅗ wide
at a 11 ~~mel~~ oClock we met 2 French in 2 canoes
lashed together Loaded with peltry &c. they
came from 80 Legges up the Kensier River where
they winterd ~~Water~~ water Strong past severall Is.d
came 15 miles encamped on the N. Side
at the uper pint of Is.d the Land is good well timber
well waterd over hunters kild one Deer
Wiensday June 6th 1804 Set out 6 oclock after
over mast mended 4 miles past a Creek on the N side
Colled Rock Creek on the Loer Side Blow Cliftu 3 miles past Saldir Creek
~~Big fish~~ on the South Side ~~Below~~ Cliftes on the Loer
Side water good the fore part of the day the latter
part Strong came 18 miles our hunters kild
one Deer encampet on the N side ~~the and way~~
~~Ios.~~ Thursday 7th June 1804 Set out 5 oclock
came 2 miles past Som prange comes out of Clifte
2 miles past a creek on the N Side colled the River
of the Big Devil

our mast off 3 miles past a Creek no [on] the South Side Called mast creek[15] ~~on the S Side no name for it but I cal it Rich Land Creek at~~ a Butifull a peas of Land as ever I saw walnut Shoger tree ash and mulber trees Level land [^]on both Sides[^] this Creek is Clear watter about 30 yardes wide one mile past a River on the N. Side colled Sedder River the Land is Level and good 4 miles past Creek Colled Zon Cer ~~Creek~~ on the S. Sid at the loer pint of IS^ld on [^]the[^] same 3 miles to a pint on the N S.^d Called Batue De harr a prarie on the S Si^d high Cliftes on the South Side ouer hunters ₓon the South Sid[^] Kild 8 Deer ₓStrong water came 10 miles[^] encamt on the South Side under the Cliftes ~~set out~~ Tuesday June 5th fair day pased Lead Creek on South Side of the River — Littel Good woman Creek on the N. Side Came 9 miles past the Creek of the Big Rock 15 ya^ds wide at a 11 ~~mil~~ oClock we met 2 French in 2 conoes lashed together Loaded with peltry &c. — they —— Came from 80 Legges [leagues] up the Kensier [Kansas] River whare

they wintered ~~wen~~ water Strong past Severall Isd. Came 15 miles Encamped on the N. Side at the uper pint of Is^d The land is Good well timberd well waterd ouer hunters Kild one Deer wensday June 6th 1804 Set out 6 oclock after ouer mast mended 4 miles past a Creek on the N Side Colled Rock Creek ₓon the Loer Side[^] Blow Clifts 3 miles past Sallin Creek ~~Big Lick~~ on the South Side ~~Below~~ Cliftes on the Loer Side water good the fore part of the day the Latter part Strong~~e~~ came 18 miles ~~e~~ouer hunters Kild one Deer encampet on the N Side ~~the midel way of IS^d~~ Sthursday 7th June 1804 Set out 5 oclock Came 2 miles past Som[s]prings Comes out of Clifte 2 miles past a Creerk on the N Side Colled the River of the Big Devil

15. Clark states he named the watercourse Mast Creek, obviously in reference to the broken mast. The captains often named geographical features after members of the expedition, an event, or a geographical feature. His name for the creek was not retained and almost surely forgotten by the time others passed through and settled in the area. The creek today is believed to be Grays Creek, Cole County, Missouri. This is a good example of what happened to the vast majority of names that the captains bestowed on geographical features. The Corps' names were unknown to most of those who followed in their wake. The failure to publish and promote the scientific data—to get the information out—for eight years, and for some data almost a century, led to their being largely forgotten or unknown. It is also worth noting the names of features, such as watercourses, that the explorers knew because of the maps they carried and the French boatmen with them who had previously traveled the river. Cedar Island and River [Creek] noted on this same day are not only an example of the party encountering features already named, but also of names that have been retained. (Moulton, 2:275, 277 n.)

one mile past a rock on the N. Side whare the fine
pictures of the Deavil and other things we
Kild 3 Rattle Snakes at that Rock 5 miles
to Creek on the N Side Colled Good woman Creek
Strong water past Several Isd. George Drwer Kild
one Bare encampet at the mouth the Land is
good well timberd &c. Friday June 8th Set out erley
this morning the day Clear wind from the west Came
5 miles past 4 Canoes lasht to gather loaded with
Bever Skins oter Skins from the littel River
thay ar 30 day from that place 5 miles
past the mouth of the Big River mine it is about
100 and 50 yardes wide about the S River on the
South Side the land is good first Rate Land well
timberd this River is navagbl for som hundred miles
aperintley water Strong past Several Isd. Came 10 miles
our hunters Kild 5 Deer encamped on the Loer
pint of an Isand on the South Side of the River
Saturday June 9th 1804 Set out after a verry hard
Rain Last night the morning Clear wind from the
Est came 5 miles past the Prarie of arrow
Is on the South Side half m. past the mouth of
arrow Creek this Creek is 8 yds wide this is a beutifull
Contry of Land the River at this place is 800 yds
wide the current Strong 3 mls past Black Bird Creek
on the N Side hagh hills on the Loer Side the Latter
part of the day Couday with Rain maid 10 miles
encampt on an Isd. in the midel of the River

Geor Drewyer or Druillard.

one mile past a rock on the N. Side whare the ~~pic~~ pictures
of the De~~a~~vil and other things we Kil^d 3 Rattle Snakes at
that Rock[16] 5 miles to Creek on the N Side Colled ~~pon~~
Good woman Creek Strong watter past severall IS^d
<u>George Druer</u> [LD: [^]<u>George Drewyer or Druillard.</u> [^]] [17]
Kild one Bar~~e~~ encampet at the mouth the Land is Good
well timberd, &c. Friday June 8th Set out erley this morning the day Clear wind from the west Came 5 miles past
2 Canoes Lasht to Gather Loaded with Bever Skins otter
Skins from the Littel River me~~en~~ thay ar 30 day ~x~coming[^]
from that place 5 miles past the mouth of the [^]Big[^]
River mine it is about 100 and 50 yardes wide a butifull
~~S~~River ~~the~~ on the South Side the Land is Good first
Rate Land well

timberd this River is navagbl for Som hundred miles
aperintley water Strong past Several IS^d Came 10 miles
ouer hunters Kild 5 Deer encamped on ~~an~~ the Loer pint
of an Isd and on the South Side of the River[18] Saturday
June 9th 1804 Set out ~~of~~ after a verry hard Rain Last night
the morning Clear wind from the Es^t cam~~c~~ 5 miles past
the Praria of arrows ~~half past 1~~ on the South Side half m.
past the mouth of arrow Creek on the South Side ~x~this
Creek is 8 yads wide[^] this is a butifull Contry of Land
the River at this place is 300 ya^ds. wide the current Strong
3 mls past Black Bird Creek on the N Side high Hills
on the Loer Side the Latter part of the day Couday with
Rain maid 10 miles encampt on an IS^d in the midel of
the River

16. The rock was near present Moniteau Creek
at Rocheport, Missouri. Clark drew figures of
the "Devil," a buffalo, and a man or manitou
in his field notes. Other journalists note that
they encountered a den of rattlesnakes here and
killed three very large ones. They were probably
timber rattlers. (Moulton, 2:283–85; 9:11.)

17. The journal's provenance and history indicate
that several people could have done this underlining and interlineation of George Drouillard's
name in red ink. But a comparison of the handwriting together with the use of red ink almost
certainly identifies the person as the inveterate
manuscript collector Lyman C. Draper. How he
acquired Floyd's journal is not definitely known,
but the most likely source is from a member of
the Clark family. It was catalogued with a group
of Clark family papers acquired (or probably
acquired) from a son or grandson of William
Clark, son of Jonathan Clark, or son of Clark's
brother-in-law William Croghan. It is known
that Draper acquired a large collection of George
Rogers Clark papers as well as some Clark and
Croghan family papers from William Croghan's
son, Dr. John Croghan, in the 1840s. Among
the Croghan portion of the collection were
several expedition date William Clark letters to
Croghan. In 1866, Draper queried Gass about
George Rogers Clark, Boone, and other frontier
figures and events. In the course of his answers,
Gass provided information about Drouillard,
indicating that Draper must have asked about
him. Thus we have a clue that Draper very possibly had Floyd's journal (the impetus for his
questioning about Drouillard) in his possession
by the mid-1860s. See the Introduction for additional information about the possible provenance
of the journal. Regarding the bears, the other
journalists list Drouillard bringing in three—a
sow and her two cubs. Floyd apparently did not
count the cubs. (Holmberg, "Getting out the
Word," pp. 15, 17 n; communication from Harry
Miller, Wisconsin Historical Society, to editor,
14 January 2004.)

18. Floyd's listing of names differs from the other
journal keepers. They identify the "Littel River"
as the Sioux River (spelled various ways). This
is the present Big Sioux River at the Iowa–South
Dakota state line. The others do not use "Big"
as part of the Mine River (present Lamine River)
name. Floyd says nothing about accompanying
Clark (as reported by Clark) on a little excursion
in the vicinity of the Missouri and Mine Rivers.
(Moulton, 2:285–87; 9:11; 11:20.)

Sunday June 10th 1804

we imbarked at the yousel over and proseded on
our Jorney 5 miles past a Creek Colled Deer Lick Creek
on the N. Side 10 yds wide the Land High
we Delayed 1½ ouers three mls past the two
Charlitons on the N. Side those Rivers mouth
neartogeathe the first 70 yds wide the Next 100 yds
wide and navagable for Some Distance in the
Cuntry halted and Capt Lewis Killed a Buck
the Current is Strong a bout this place Came
12 miles past Severall Islds our hunters Killed 3 Deer
                                        and well watered
incamped on the South Side at a prara this prara is High we

monday June 11th 1804 day Clear wind from the N. W.
                                      nothing
ouer hunters Killed a Bear and two

monday June 11th 1804 a Day Clear wind from the
N. West Lay By all all Day on account of the
wind the Latter part of the day Clouday our
hunters Kiled 2 Bars Deer Tuesday June 12 1804
we
Set out at the ufial over and the day Clear
wind from the west Came 4 miles past a Creek on
the S. Side Colled Plumb Creek about 20 yds wide
the timber in this Bottoms is Cotten wood
          miles
2 when we met two 5 Cannoes from the Soux
                                        and Greaw
         nations Loaded with pettry, thay have
been 13 mounthes up the missouri River
Delayed ½ day with the French Baught Some
our hunters Did one French man hiard to go with us up the
tallow of not Rottin last night missouri who can Speck the Differn
          them incamped on the N. Side the
Land Good Bottom Wensday June 13th 1804
Set out at 6 oclock and Came 1½ miles
                                        past

[^]Sunday June 10th 1804[^] we imbarked at the yousel ouer
and proseded on our Jorney 5 miles past a Creek Colled
Deer Lick Creek on the N Side 10 yads wide the Land
High ~~Hil~~ Delayed 1 ½ ouers three mls past the two Ɛ
Charlitons on the N. Side thoses Rivers mouth near toge-
athe the first 70 ya^ds wide the Next 100 yads wide and
navagable for Some Distance in the Cuntry halted and
Capt Lewis Killed a Buck the Current is Strong a bout this
place Came 12 miles past Severall IS^d ouer hunters Killed
3 Deer incamped on the South Side at a priara this priara
is High well ₓand well waterd &c.[^] ~~monday June 11th-
1804 day Clear wind from the NW^t~~ ouer hunters Kilded
~~2 Bare and two Deer~~ [^]nothing[^] Monday June 11th 1804
Ɛ Day Clear wind from the N. West Lay By all all Day
on account of the

wind the Latter part of the day Clouday ouer hunters
Kiled 2 Bar & 2 Deer Tuesday June 12 1804 [^]we[^] Set
out at the Usial ouer ~~and~~ the day Clear wind from the west
Came 4 miles past a Creek on the S. Side Colled <u>Plumb
Creek</u>[19] a bout 20 yads wide the timber in this Bottoms
is Cotten wood 2 ₓmiles[^] when we met ~~two~~ 5 Caunoes
from the ~~Shoue~~ [^]~~Sue~~[^] <u>Soux</u> ~~nathion~~ nations Loaded with
peltry and Greese thay have been 13 mounthes up the
missorea River Delayed ½ day with the French, Baught
Some tallow of them [^]ouer hunters Did not Rettern Last
night one French man hiard to go with us up the missorea
who can Speak the Difernt [languages or dialects][^][20]
encamped on the N. Side the Land Good Bottom wensday June 13th 1804 Set out at 6 oclock and Came 1 ½
miles past

19. A hand other than Floyd's underlined "Plumb
Creek" and "Soux." Clark is a possibility, as is
Nicolas Biddle (who also used red ink as well
as regular) if he had access to Floyd's journal.
Other possibilities are James D. Butler, the
journal's first editor, and Reuben Gold Thwaites,
its second editor; but the most likely candidate
would seem to be Draper if it is accepted that he
used regular ink in addition to red ink. If first
Lewis and then Clark retained their deceased
sergeant's journal, the possibility exists that
Biddle had possession of it while he worked on
the official expedition history. If so, it is possible
that he made some of the underscoring, but a
comparison of words and phrases so marked in
the Floyd journal failed to find a corresponding
match in Clark's and Ordway's journals, both
of which Biddle definitely had in his possession
and marked in. Some underlined words do
match up between the Clark and Floyd journals
but not all three. Therefore, the best evidence
indicates Draper did the underlining, using
black/brown ink as well as red.

20. Floyd and others always note encountering
boats coming down the river. From information
recorded, it is clear that they talked with the
travelers. This entry is a good example, noting
not only that they spent half a day with the
Frenchmen learning what they could expect to
encounter upriver, but that the captains hired
Pierre Dorion Sr. of that party as an interpreter
for their anticipated encounter with American
Indian nations. Clark explains this (as he usually did the day's events) much more fully than
Floyd and the other journalists. (See Moulton,
2:295 n, for more information on Dorion.)

past a Creek on the N Side Colleded River missorea
past the Creek above a Large Praria of Good Land on the N Side
at this Prarie antient Missourie Iordianes had
a village at this place 300 of them ware killed
by the Saukus in former times a fair day past the Grand River on
the N. Side the Land is Level on Both Sides a hansom
a handsom Prarie on the Loer Side of it water Strong
past Several Isd. Came 10 miles the Grand River
is about 200 and 50 yards wide and Boates Can
go for som hundreds of miles up it our hunters
killed yesterday and to day 1 Bar, 2 Deer encampted
at the mouth of the Grand River on the N Side off the River
Thursday June 14th 1804 we Set out

at the usuel ouer and proseded on our Iorney
day Clear water Strong came 3 miles met 2 Canoes
with 3 French men and one Malcatto Negro from the Poncye
Nations they have ben up 3 years with the Indianes,
2 of them is half preades of the poncas. past a Creek
on the N Side Colleded the Snake Creek it is about
25 yads wide a noted place whare Indianes Peopel
of Differnt nations Craff to go to ware they
Say that thar is hundreds of Snakes at this
place our hunters killed one Deer encamped on the N
Side of the River the land is good about hear the Chief
of the timber is cotten wood. Friday June 15th
we Set out at 5 oclock after much Feteages

past a Creek on the N Side Colleded River missorea[21]
Just above ₓthe Creek₍^₎ a Large Praria of Good Land
on the N Side at this Prarre Antunt [ancient] <u>Missourie
Indianes</u> had a <u>village at this place 300 of them were
killed by the Saukus</u> ₐ<u>in former times.</u>₍^₎[22] a fair day past
the Grand River on the N. Side the Land is Level on Both
Sides a̶ ̶h̶a̶n̶d̶s̶ a handsom Prarie on the Loer Side of it
water Strong past Severral IS^d Came 10 miles the Grand
River is about 200 and 50 yads wide and Boates Can Go
for Som hundreds of miles up it[23] ouer hunters Killed
yesterday and to day 1 Bar, 2 Deer encamped at the
mouth of the Grand River on the N Side of the River
w̶e̶ ̶S̶e̶t̶ <u>Thursday June</u>[24] 14th 1804 we Set out

at the usuel ouer and proseded on our Jorney day Clear
water Strong Came 3 miles p̶a̶s̶t̶ met 2 Conoes with
3 French men and one Negro ₍^₎[WC: Mallatto]₍^₎ from
the Poneye Nation̶s̶ They have ben up 3 years with the
Indianes 2 of them is half preades [breeds] of the poncas.[25]
past a Creek on the N. Side Colled the Snake Creek it is
about 25 ya^ds wide a noted place whare Indinanes C̶r̶o̶u̶s̶s̶
of Differnt nations Cross to Go to ware they Say that thar
is hundreds of Snakes at this place[26] ouer hunters killed
one Deer encamped on the N Side of the River the Land
is good about hear the Chief of the timber is Cotten wood.
<u>Friday June 15</u>^th we Set out at 5 oclock o̶f̶ ̶t̶e̶ after much
f̶e̶t̶e̶g̶e̶d̶ Feteaged

21. This passage is confusing. Floyd either failed to record or misunderstood the name of the creek he calls "River missorea." Clark records the two creeks coming in as the "Creeks of the round Bend" (of the Missouri) in his field notes and later as "round bend creek" in his fair copy journal. Ordway records the latter name. Floyd also misplaces his "x" insertion mark, meaning apparently to insert "the Creek" after "above" rather than before it. (Moulton, 2:295-96; 9:13.)

22. It is believed that Draper did the red underlining. (See notes 17 and 19.) The caret, rather than Floyd's more commonly used "x" indicating a word or phrase to be inserted, most likely was added by Clark, Draper, or other person with access to the journal. The Missouria (or Missouri) Indians lived at the confluence of the Missouri and Grand Rivers in the late seventeenth century when first noted by Europeans. After being almost annihilated by the Sauk Indians in the late eighteenth century, they drifted up the Missouri and allied themselves with their relatives the Oto. Their economy was based on hunting and farming. The Sauk lived along the Mississippi River in northwestern Illinois and eastern to central Iowa. They were allied with the Fox Indians. They hunted and farmed and, like many tribes, sought to extend their control over additional land for hunting and trapping. This resulted in conflict with the Missouria in the late eighteenth century as they expanded southwest. The Corps did not encounter the Sauk, but they are frequently mentioned in Lewis and Clark's post-expedition Indian affairs reports. Their power was not broken until the 1832 Black Hawk War. This passage is a good example of Floyd (and the other journalists) incorporating information gleaned from travelers they encountered, the French boatmen with them, and other sources into their journals. (Moulton, 2:295-96, 299 n; Lamar, p. 574.)

23. Floyd differs greatly in his estimate of the width of the Grand River from Clark (Ordway, Gass, and Whitehouse do not comment on it). Clark states it is about 120 yards wide in his field notes and lowers it to 80-100 yards wide in his fair copy journal. He also gives no estimate of the length of the Grand, writing only that it is navigable for pirogues a "great distance." Since Floyd rather consistently agrees with Clark's estimates of distances (perhaps even getting them from him), his estimate of the Grand is in great disagreement. If feet instead of yards are used, then his estimate is more in line with Clark's. It is a little surprising that Clark—who read and made not only additions to but also corrections in Floyd's journal—did not correct or comment on this apparent error and contradiction. Floyd's source for the Grand being navigable for hundreds of miles is unknown. Perhaps it is his version of Clark's "great distance" or it was gathered from one of their French boatmen or travelers encountered. (Moulton, 2:296.)

(continued on page 57)

of yesterdays worke pased a Creek on the South Side
Coleded Indian Creek it is about 15 yards wide good Level
Land over hunters killed 4 Bar 3 Deer Strong water
Encampt on the N Side opset to cintint
old villag of Missures indians but the
~~village family lived the day but the~~
Saukies bong two trobelsom for them was forst to move
and take protections under the Gran ossage as
they war Redused Small   the river is 3 mile
hands in a prarie as ~~ever by~~ eney Indian said wide
hear
Saturday JUNE 16th wes Set out of at 8 oclock
day Clouday with rain nothing Remarkeble to Day water verry
Strong past one place whare the water Roles over the Sand
withe grait fall and verry Daingeres for Boats to pass
past Severall Isld. maid 10 miles over hunters Did not Return
Last night Encamped on the N Side of the River the
Land is good hear and well timberd Sunday June 17th
we Renued our Journey much fetegude of yesterdays
worke Came one mil encamped for the purpos of
maken...ones for our Boat and make a rope for the purpos
of towen on the North Side of the River our hunters
Returnd and killed on Bar one Deer and found a Stray
horse who had Been Lost for Sometime nothing Remark b g
to day Monday JUNE 18th Clouday ~~day th~~ with Rain
and Thunder and wind ~~from~~ from the Est

of yesterdays worke[27]   pased a Creek on the South Side
Colleded Indian Creek ~~no~~ it is about 15 yards wide
Good Level Land ~~enca~~ ouer hunters Killed 4 Bars and
ᴧ3 Deer[ᴧ] Strong water encamp on the N Side opset to
antint ~~Indian village fomley lived the ossage but the~~ [ᴧ]old
villag of Missures Indians but the —[ᴧ] Saukus beng two
trobelsom ᴧfor them[ᴧ] was forst to move and take protections under the Gran ossags as they war Reᵈused Small[28]
handson a prarie as ever ~~lay~~ eney man saw ᴧthe river is
3 miles wide hear[ᴧ] Saurday June 16ᵗʰ wes Set out ~~of~~ at
8 oclock day Clouday with rain nothing Remarkeble to
[ᴧ]Day[ᴧ] water verry Srong past one place whare the water
Roles over the Sand

withe grait fall and verry Daingeris for Boats to pass[29]
past Severall ISlᵈ Maid 10 miles ouer hunters Did not
Return Last night encamped on the N Side of the River
the Land is good hear and well timberd Sunday June 17ᵗʰ
we Renued our Journey much fetegeued of yesterdays
work Came one mil encamped for the purpos of maken
ores for ouer Boat and make a rope for the pursos of towen
on the North Side of the River ouer hunters Returnd and
Killed on Bar one Deer and found a Stray Horse who had
Been Lost for Sometime nothing Remarkesᴧble[ᴧ] to day[30]
Monday June 18ᵗʰ Clouday ~~day sh~~ with Rain and thunder and wind ~~N. w~~ from the Esᵗ

(continued from page 55)

24. This is the first of a number of entry dates
underlined by an unknown hand. It is unlikely
that Floyd underlined them. The most likely
people are Clark, Biddle, or Draper.
25. In reviewing Floyd's journal, Clark revised
Negro to "Mallatto," meaning of course *mulatto.*
Clark makes no comment about the racial and
ethnic composition of the group or its members.
Ordway states there were four Frenchmen in the
group. Therefore, Floyd is much more specific
in noting that one man was black and two of
the three Frenchmen were half Indian—Ponca
Indians, a neighboring tribe of the Pawnee
(Floyd's "Poneye"). Moulton states that Floyd
may have meant they were Pawnee, not Ponca.
It would seem that they could have been Ponca.
Both were semi-sedentary tribes living in the
vicinity of the confluence of the Missouri and
Platte Rivers. The Corps did not encounter
either tribe. Floyd's simple mention of "water
Strong" indicates the velocity and dangerous
nature of the Missouri's current but fails to
relate several serious river incidents regarding
the keelboat. His "hard" water and "fast" water
observations also indicate particularly bad
stretches of the river. Ordway is generally silent
on the subject also, but Clark and Whitehouse
do relate the incidents. (Moulton, 2:296, 300,
302; 11:23–24.)
26. Snake Creek, Carroll County, Missouri, is
probably the present name of their Wa Kenda
Creek. Clark is the only journalist to relate
Drouillard's story of hearing a snake making
gobbling noises like a turkey. Drouillard also
reported that when he fired his gun, it gobbled
louder. Clark wrote that one of the Frenchmen
also told such a story. (Moulton, 2:300–1.)
27. This is classic Floyd understatement. Both he
and Ordway make little mention of the dangers
and hardships of the journey. The Corps had
narrowly escaped disaster when the keelboat
struck a sand bar and began to turn in the current. Clark reported that only the extraordinary
exertions of the men had prevented the boat
from turning, which would have resulted in it
overturning. Only Floyd's mention of "Strong"
water in his 14 June entry and comment that
the men were still tired on the fifteenth after
their exertions of the day before hint at this
near disaster. (Moulton, 2:300.)
28. Clark explains this more fully. As a result
of the Sauk's invasion of their homeland, the
Missouria first took refuge with the Little Osage.
When the Sauk then forced both those tribes
to abandon their villages, the Little Osage and
some Missouria settled with the Great Osage
and most of the Missouria merged with the Oto.
(Moulton, 2:302–3.)
29. This was the third consecutive day that the
Corps encountered particularly difficult and
dangerous river conditions. Clark noted that
this stretch of the Missouri was recognized

(continued on page 59)

the Land at this Bottom is ~~Land~~ Good Land the timber
is Cotten wood ouer hunters killed one Bar 5 Deer
~~noth~~ nothing worth Relating Tusday June 19th
Set out at 8 oclock day Clouday wind from the
Est Sailed past a Creek on the South Side Colleded
Labor Creek it is about 40 yards wide and
Clear water below High Hills good Land well
timberd past Several IS's Strong water Came
13 miles encamped on the South Side of the
River our hunters Did not Return Last night
Wensday June 20th 1804 Set out ~~as yousel late~~
Clouday day Rain Srong ~~lak~~ water past Several IS's Came
12 miles our Hunters Did not Return Last night

encamped on an IS's in the middel of the River
Thursday June 21th Set out at 7 oclock
Clear day past Creek on the South Side Colleded
Pellcau Creeke thay Com in at the opper point of opset the middel of IS's
~~it IS's~~ the water at this IS's is varry Strong the Land
is good and ~~well~~ High timberd on the South Side the Land
high that on the N is Low ~~Botton~~ Land the timber is Cotton
wood water Strong past Several IS's Came 9 miles our
hunters killed one Der encamped on the South Side
at the opper pint of IS's the Land is Law that on the N
is High Land Friday June 22d Set out at 7 oclock after a verry hard
Storm thunder ~~and from the N E~~ and Rain wind
~~from the West~~ proceeded on under a gentle Breeze from the S W past
~~from the N E~~ past a Creek on the South Side Colleded the Little
Five Creek it Comes in opset the middel

the Land at this Bottom ~~Land~~ [^]is[^] Good Land [^]the[^]
timbr is Cotten wood ouer hunters Killed one Bar 5 Deer
~~th~~ nothing worth Relating Tusday June 19ᵗʰ Set out at
8 oclock day Clouday wind from the E Esᵗ Sailed past a
Creek on the South Side Colleded tabor Creek it is a bout
40 yards wide and Clear water below High Hills good
Land well timberd past Several ISᵈs Strong water Came
13 miles encamped on the South Side of the River ouer
hunters Did not Return Last night Wensday June 20ᵗʰ
1804 Set out ~~as yousel late~~ Clouday [^]day[^] Rain, Srong
~~fats~~ [fast] water past Several ISᵈ Came 12 miles ouer
Hunters Did not Return Last night

encamped on an ISᵈ in the middel of the River Thursday
June 21th Set out at 7 oclock Clear day past 2 Creeks
on the South Side Collede Deulau Creeks³¹ they com in
~~at the opper pint of the ISᵈ~~ [^]opset the middel of ISᵈ[^] the
water at this ISᵈs is verry Strong the Land is Good and
well timberd [^]~~High~~[^] on the South Side the Land high
that on the N. is ~~Bottom~~ [^]Low[^] Land the timber is
Cotton wood water Strong past Sevral ISᵈ came 9 miles
ouer hunters killed one Deer encamped on the South Side
at the opper pint of ISᵈ the Land is Low that on the N. is
High Land Friday June 22d Set out ∧at 7 oclock[^] after
a verry hard Storm thunder ~~wind from the N. E.~~ and Rain
wind ~~from the N.E. past~~ [^][WC: from the West, proceeded
on under a gentle Breeze from the N.W. passd][^]³² a Creek
on the South Side Colleded the Littel Fire Creek it Comes
in opset the middel

(continued from page 57)

as the worst part of the river. Whitehouse
noted that they had to cut trees down along
the riverbank in order to tow the boat upstream.
(Moulton, 2:302; 11:25.)

30. Clark had walked on shore part of the previous
day, in part to scout for timber to make oars of
which he stated they were "much in want of."
He called their encampment "Rope walk Camp"
in his field notes regarding making a towline
(as well as oars). Ordway wrote that they got
enough timber for twenty oars. Whitehouse
not only named the camp and number of oars
made, but also stated they made six hundred
feet of rope out of bearskins. Regarding the
horse, Clark noted that it was young and fat
and must have gotten away from an Indian
raiding party that usually crossed the river at
that place. The explorers remained in camp
to finish the oars and rope on the eighteenth,
and no doubt to rest from their recent river
experiences and exertions. Clark noted that
several men were ill with dysentery and that
about two-thirds had boils and skin ulcers.
(Moulton, 2:305-7; 9:14; 11:25-26.)

31. The journalists all give various spellings for this
creek or creeks. Ordway and Gass list one creek,
while Floyd and Clark list two (Whitehouse is
silent on the matter). Clark says they are named
for a Frenchman. Moulton interprets Floyd's
spelling of the creek to be Deubau with a "b"
rather than an "l." (Moulton, 2:312-14; 9:15,
382; 10:16.)

32. This is the first lengthy insertion by Clark. It is
not known if he was reviewing Floyd's journal
regularly and inserted this at the time or if he
did so when he kept Floyd's journal for him on
25 and 26 June due to Floyd apparently having
a sore hand (perhaps a blister, skin ulcer, or
boil?). The addition on this day is done as an
interlineation, which indicates that Clark was
reading the journal a day or more after Floyd
had written it rather than the same day.

of a Small Id; on the south side Strong water Came 9 miles
encamped on the South Side at a Prarie on the N. this Prarie is colled Fire
Side Comes in a Creek Colled the Big Fire Creek
the Creek is about 50 yards wide and High Land

Saturday June 23d a Small Breze from the N. W Set
out day Couday Set out at 5 Oclock day Couday Came
3 miles landed on acount of the wind from the N.W.
armes and ammunition inspcted examined all in good order
Capt Clark want hunting did not Return last night
encamped on and Sunday June 24
all Day & night clear wind from we continued on this Island
Cap Return erley in the morning Killed
one Deer our Hunter Killed one Bear 4 Deer they
encamped on an Id on the N Side we Crossed a
land bar where the water was so shoal that we were obleged
to haul over the boat, encamped on the S. Side below an Island

Sunday June 24th 1804 Set out verley at
5 Oclock A.m wind from the N. E. Sailed Day
Clear passed a Creek on the South Side colled Hay
Creek it is about 40 yards wide Clear water Land
High and good well timberd Delayed 2 ours to Dry som
meat Capt. Lewis & my self went Hunting Kild one Deer
& a Turkey passed a Creek on the North Side colled Charriton Creek
it is about 30 yards wide passed a Creek on the
Same Side colled the Creek of the Bad Rock it
is not far below the other it is about 15 yards wide
the Land is High and well timberd our Hunters
Killed 8 Deer water good made 13 miles encamped on the
South Side the Land is good first Rate Land, On this sd
of the river we above feeding on the Bank & the adjacent
Monday Prarie immence Heerds of Deer, Bear is also plenty in the
bottom,

of a Small IS^d on the South Side Strong water Came
9 miles encamped on the Southe Side at a Prarie ˌthis
Prarie is Colled Fire₍ᴧ₎³³ on the N. Side Comes in a
Creek Colled the Big Fire Creek the Creek is about
50 yards wide and High Land Saturday June 23^thd a
Small Brese from the N. W ~~Set out day Clouday~~ Set
out at 5 oclock day Couday Came 3 miles Landed on
acount of the wind from the N. W. armes and amunition
~~examend~~ ₍ᴧ₎enspcted₍ᴧ₎ all in good order Capt Clark want
hunting Did not Return Last night ~~encamped on an IS^d~~
~~₍ᴧ₎ouer Hunters Killed 2 Deer₍ᴧ₎ Sunday June 24th Set~~
~~out day Clear wind from~~ [WC: we Continued on this
Island all Day & night]³⁴ but Returnd erley in the morning
Killed one Deer ouer Hunter Killed one Bear 4 Deer
[WC: ˌthey₍ᴧ₎] encamped on an IS^d on the N Side [WC:
~~we Crossed a Sand bar where the water was So Shoal that~~
~~we were were obliged to Haul over the boat, Incamped~~
~~on the L. Side below an Island]³⁵~~

Sunday June 24th 1804 Set out ~~verley~~ at 5 oclock A.m.
wind from the N.E. Sailed Day — Clear passed a Creek
on the South Side Colled Hay Creek it is about 40 yards
wide Clear water Land High and Good well timber^d
Delayed 2 ouers to Dry Some meat Capt Lewis [WC:
ˌ& my Self₍ᴧ₎]³⁶ went hunting Kild one Deer [WC: ˌ&
a Turkey₍ᴧ₎] passed a Creek on the North Side Colled
Charriton Creek it is about 30 yards wide passed a Creek
on the Same Side Colled the Creek of the Bad Rock³⁷ it is
not far below the other it is about 15 yards wide the Land
is High and well timberd ouer Hununters Killed 8 Deer
water Good made 13 miles encamped on the South Side
the Land is Good first Rate Land, [WC: On this p^t of the
River we observe feeding on the Banks & the adjacent
Praries imencce Hurds of Deer, Bear is also plenty in the
bottoms,]³⁸ ~~monday~~

33. This stretch of the river had continued to be
quite difficult to ascend. Only Clark and Whitehouse give any specifics to truly indicate just
how difficult it was. Clark would return to the
Fire Prairie in the summer of 1808 and super-
vise the construction of Fort Osage. On a back
page of his journal for this date, Floyd listed
his squad and made notations regarding guard
duty assignments (see note 97).

34. In observing the placement of Clark's addition,
he easily could have added this while briefly
keeping Floyd's journal for him. It begins at
the end of a sentence on one line and is written
in the space above Floyd's next line. Clark's
account of his hunting venture is quite interesting. (Moulton, 2:317–19.)

35. Clark's addition of a line again comes at a place
where there was space to make additional comments. He was not keeping Floyd's journal yet
so he probably added this when keeping it for
him just a couple of days later. Why it is crossed
out is unknown.

36. Floyd's Hay Creek was Hay Cabin Creek
according to Clark and Ordway, Straw Hill
River to Whitehouse, and Depie Creek to Gass
(which Moulton notes might relate to the French
de paille meaning "of straw"). It soon became
known as the Little Blue River, the name it
retains today. Floyd's brevity again sacrifices
interesting information. Clark's insertion of
Floyd's name in the first-person and his own
mention of it in his journal place Floyd out
hunting with Lewis. Ordway records that Lewis
went hunting and killed a deer and a turkey
but makes no mention of Floyd being with him.
Since Floyd does not discuss their excursion
and Lewis apparently was not keeping a journal during this part of the trip, no details—like
those for Clark's hunting adventure—are known.
(Moulton, 2:319, 320 n; 9:16; 10:16; 11:29–30.)

37. Floyd is the only journalist to call this particu-
lar creek Bad Rock. The others call it various
names. It probably is present Big Shoal Creek,
indicating the rocks and shallows there that the
Corps noted. (Moulton, 2:320–21.)

38. This is again added by Clark in space at the
bottom of a page, most likely while reviewing
Floyd's journal while keeping it for him on
25–26 June.

Monday June 25th we set out at 8 oclock after the
Fague was gon, pass a Coal Mine on the South Side above a Small
Island, a Small Creek below which takes its name from the bank of
Coal, and large Creek at about one Mile higher up the river on
the Same Side Calleas (un batteur La benne River) passed Several
Small Islands on the South Side, Some hard water, & camped on a Small
Istand near the North Side Cap. Lewis Killed a Rabit, A Fielas a Deer this evening
our flanking party did not join us this evening / my hand is painfull)

Tuesday June 26th we set out early proceeded on passed a Island on
this the South Side, back of this Island a large Creek coms in called
Blue water Creek (Riur Le Bleue) The Hills or High lands on the River
which we passed last evening & this morning on L.S. is higher than
usial from 160, to 180 feet encampt at the mouth of the Kansas
River in the print it comes in on the South Side

WENES day June 27th Stayed Lay By all
this day oerer Hunters Killed 5 Deer

Thursday June 28 the Lay By all that Day the
Kansas River is 30.4 yards wide at the mouth
the Land is good on Booth sides of these Rivers and well
timberd well waterd Friday June 29 Set out
at Half past 4. oclock om from the Kansas River
proceeded on passed a run on the South Side, at the
mouth of Kansas River arms and amunition.
Inespected all in good order encampt on the N side
late in the evning Saturday June 3t 1804
Set out verry early this morning Saw a Wolf on
the Sind Bare passed the tittet River platte on the
N. Side it is about 100 yards wide Clear water High
Land on the Lear Side of it on this River it is sayed
that thare is a nomber of falls on it fitting for
for

Monday June 25th we Set ou at 8 oclock after the Fague
was Gon, [WC: pass a Coal mine on the South Side above
a Small Island, a Small Creek below which takes its name
from the bank of Coal, and large Creek at about one Mile
higher up the River on the Same Side Called (un batteur
La benne River)][39] [WC: passed several small Islands on
the South Side. Some hard water, & camped on a small
Island near the North Side Cap[t] Lewis Killed a Rabit,
R. Fields a Deer this evin[g] our flanking party did not
join us this evening (my hand is painfull)]

[WC: Tuesday June 26th we Set out early proceeded on
passed a Island on the the South Side, back of this Island
a large Creek coms in call[d] Blue Water Creek (River Le
Bléue) The Hills or High lands on the River which we
passed last evening & this morning on L.S. is higher than
usial from 160, to 180 feet.][40] encampt at the mouth of the
Kansas River in the pint it comes in ~~oppeset~~ on the Southe
ᴀSide[^] ~~th~~ wensday June 27th ~~Stayed hear~~ Lay By all ~~day~~
~~Clouday~~ ᴀthis day[^] ouer Hunters Killed 5 Deer

Thursday June 28th Lay By all that Day the Kansas River
is 200 30 ¼ yards wide at the mouth the Land is Good
on Booth Sides ᴀof[^] thes Rivers and well timberd well
waterd Friday June 29 Set out at Half past 4 oclock Pm
from the Kansas River proceeded on passed ~~R~~ a run on
the South Side, at the [^]ᴀt[^] mouth of Kansas River armes
and amunition enspected all in Good order encampt on
the N. Side Late in the evning[41] Saturday June 30th 1804
Set out verry early this morning Saw a wolf on the Sind
Bare passed the Littel River platte on the N. Side it is
about 100 yards wide[42] Clear water High Land on the
Loer Side of it on this River it is Sayed that thare is a
number of ~~fowl~~ falls on it fitting forer [^]for[^]

39. Previous editors have identified this passage
as being written by Clark. It is clearly in his
usual handwriting. All the journalists spell
"La benne" different ways but only in Floyd's
does "un batteur" and "river" appear. Since
Clark seems to clearly be writing this entry,
it seems unusual that it varies from his own
journal entry of that date. (Moulton, 2:321.)

40. Previous editions of Floyd's journal have
identified the second part of the 25 June and
most of the 26 June entries as being in an unknown hand. I think it is also in Clark's hand
but in an altered style for some reason. The
writing is consistent with handwriting in letters
he wrote during the expedition. Since he writes
in Floyd's voice, the parenthetical statement
"my hand is painful" could be an admission
to explain why Floyd is not keeping his own
journal or to explain his own altered hand. If
the latter, he does not mention it in his own
journal for his 25 or 26 June entries, and certain
letters and words compare favorably with that
portion of Floyd's. Some of the statistics and
names are also the same: Blue Water Creek, river
Le Bléue (although there are slight differences),
and 160 to/and 180 feet. Also, note the use of
L.S. for larboard side, which only Clark used
of the known journal keepers at this time.
(Moulton, 2:321–24; Clark, pp. 70–73.)

41. The reasons for the late start were Lewis and
Clark taking observations and the court martial
of John Collins and Hugh Hall. The charges
were brought by Floyd. Collins was found guilty
of getting drunk on whiskey under his care
while on guard duty and also letting Hall get
some. Hall was found guilty of taking whiskey
against orders. Collins's sentence was one hundred lashes and Hall's was fifty. The punish-
ments were given at 3:30 that afternoon, at
which time the party paraded for inspection—
perhaps Floyd's mention of arms and ammunition being inspected. Whitehouse noted that
there was a concern that the Kansa (or Kaw)
Indians, who lived up the Kansas River and
were believed to be warlike, might attack. This
might have been a reason for the inspection also.
Floyd says nothing about another close call by
the keelboat involving a sand bar and sawyer.
(Moulton, 2:328–30; 11:32.)

42. Floyd, Ordway, and Clark all differ on the
width of the mouth of the Little Platte River.
Ordway states fifty yards, Clark seventy yards,
and Floyd one hundred yards. Either they were
not comparing entries or were sticking with
their own estimates.

mills the Land is Rolling eausept on the South Side
the Land is Low that on the N is the same

Sunday July 1th 1804 Set out Clear day passed
Small Creek on the South Side Colled Biscuit C: High Land —
passed a Creek on the S. Side Colled Frog Tree Creek a Pond
on the N S. Colled the Same name Good water made
12½ miles Campt on an Is.d near the South Side our
Flanken party Did not Joine Last euning

    monday July 2.d Set out verry early this
morning passed on the Left of the Is.d parques
High butifule Situation on the South Side the
Land indifferent Lands a Creek comes in on the

N Side colled parkques Creek passed a Creek on the N.
Side called Turkey Creek High Lande came 18 miles
Campt on the N Side on the So th Side w.d a old Trading
fort in our tour the old kansus villag on the Back of this villag
is High Hills of Prarie Land of on the South Side
was a old French Villege who had setled hear to protect
the Trade of this nation in the valley the kansas
Had a village between tow points of High Land Prarie Land
a Handsom situation for a town   Tuesday July 3.th
Set out verry erly this morning under a Jantel
Breeds from the South found a Stray Horse on the
South Side they had Ben Lost for Som time
water verry strong So hard that we could hardley
Stem it came 11 miles Campt on the South Side the
Land is verry murdey

mills the land is Rolling campt on the South Side the
Land is Low that on the N is the Same⁴³ Sunday July 1ᵗʰ
1804 Set out Clear day passed Small Creek on the South
Side Colled Biscuit C. High Land — passed a Creek on
the S. Side colled Frog Tree Creek a Pond on the N S.
Colled the Same name Good water made 12 ½ miles
Campᵗ on an ISᵈ Near the South Side ouer Flanken party
Did not Join us Last evning⁴⁴ monday July 2ᵈ Set out
verry early this morning passed on the Left of the ISᵈ
parques High butifule Situation on the South Side the
Land indifferent Lands a Creek Comes in on the S̶o̶

N Side colled parkques ∧Creek₍∧₎ passed a creek on the
N — Side called — Turkey Creek High Landes came
10 miles campt on the N Side, o̶n̶ ̶t̶h̶e̶ ̶S̶o̶u̶t̶h̶ ̶S̶i̶d̶e̶ ̶w̶a̶s̶ ̶a̶ ̶o̶l̶d̶
F̶r̶e̶n̶c̶h̶ ̶f̶o̶r̶t̶ ̶i̶n̶ ̶f̶o̶r̶m̶e̶r̶ ̶t̶i̶m̶e̶s̶ ̶t̶h̶e̶ ̶o̶l̶d̶ ̶K̶a̶n̶s̶a̶s̶ ̶v̶i̶l̶l̶a̶g̶ ̶o̶n̶ ̶t̶h̶e̶,̶
₍∧₎o̶n̶ ̶t̶h̶e̶₍∧₎ ̶B̶a̶c̶k̶ ̶o̶f̶ ̶t̶h̶i̶s̶ ̶v̶i̶l̶l̶a̶g̶ ̶i̶s̶ ̶H̶i̶g̶h̶ ̶H̶i̶l̶l̶s̶ ̶o̶f̶ ̶P̶r̶a̶r̶a̶e̶ ̶L̶a̶n̶d̶
T̶ on the South Side was a old French Fort who had Setled
hear to protect the ∧to protect₍∧₎ Trade of this nation in the
valley the Kansas Had a village betwen tow pints of High
L̶a̶n̶d̶s̶ Praria Land a Handsom Situation for a town⁴⁵
S̶ Tuesday July 3ᵈᵗʰ Set out verry erley this morning under
a Jentel Breas from the South found a H̶o̶r̶s̶e̶ Stray Horse
on the South Side Havg Had Ben Lost for Som time
water verry Strong So Hard that we Could Hardley Stem
it⁴⁶ Came 10 miles Campt on the South Side ∧the₍∧₎ Land
is verry mirey

43. Floyd makes no mention of the keelboat's mast
being broken by a small tree hanging over the
river as they put in to the bank. Only Ordway
mentioned it. (Moulton, 9:19.)

44. Only Clark notes that an alarm was sounded
the previous night and that "all prepared for
action." This and other mentions indicate
the growing awareness and precautions for
a prepared defense as the party ascended the
Missouri. Perhaps Floyd's reference to their
hunters as a flanking party is a reference to
this heightened caution. Ordway refers to
the flanking party not rejoining them in his
2 July entry. The hunters came in on 2 July so
Ordway might have intended this statement for
his 1 July entry, or another party was out reconnoitering for defense that no one mentioned,
which seems unlikely. (Moulton, 2:338; 9:19.)

45. This was Fort de Cavagnial (or Cavagnolle),
built by the French in 1744 and abandoned in
1764 when France ceded Louisiana to Spain.
Its presence near the old Kansa village Floyd
mentions was an effort to control trade with
the Kansa and the Osage. The two tribes abandoned their villages in this area because of
hostile incursions by the Sauk and the Iowa.
It was just north of present Fort Leavenworth,
Kansas. Floyd makes no mention of the difficult
river travel encountered that day or of putting
up a new mast. (Moulton, 2:340–42, 343 n; 9:19;
11:33-34.)

46. All the journalists mention the horse, although
its color ranged from white to gray. Clark notes
it was lost by the Indians and was fat and gentle.
It was sent ahead to join the party's other horses
traveling along the south (or west) bank. He
says nothing of the abandoned French trader's
house. Floyd is the only one to mention the
water being hard to proceed against that day.
Clark and Whitehouse note such current in
their 2 July entries. (Moulton, 2:343–44.)

Wendday July 4th 1804 Set out Very erly
this morning passed the mouth of a Beyeu leading from a lake
on the N: Side this lake is large and was once the Bead
of the River it reaches Parrelel with for Several miles,
Came to on the South Side to Dine rest a Short time
a Snake Bit Jo. Fieldes on the Side of the foot
which Sweled much apply Bark to Coonsurd passed
a Creek on the South Side about 15 yards wide
Coming out of an extensive Prarie as the Creek has
no name and this Day is the 4th of July we name this
Independance Creek above this Creek the wood Land
is about 200 yards Back of those wood is an extensive
Pruria open and High whigh may be Seen Six or Seven
below Grate number of Goslins to day nearley Grown

the Last mintioned prarie I Call Jo. Fieldes Snake
prarie Capt Lewis walked on Shore we Camped
at one of the Butifules Praries I ever Saw open and
butifulley Devided with Hills and valleys all
presenting Themselves Thursday July 5th 1804 Set out
erley this morning Swam over Stray Horse a Cross
the River to Join our other Horses prossed on for under
the Banks of the old Kansas village formaley
Stood in 1724 the cause of thes Indians moving
from this place I cant Larn but natureley
Concluded that wars has reduced thair nation and
Compelled them to Retire further in to the Plaines
with a view of Defending themselves and

wensday July 4th 1804 Set out verry erley this morning
passed the mouth of a Beyew leading from a lake on the
N. Side this Lake is Large and was~~e~~ once the Bead of the
River it reaches Parrelel ~~with~~ for Several miles Came
to on the South Side to Dine rest a Short time a Snake
Bit Jo. Fieldes on the Side of the foot ~~swe~~ which Sweled
much apply Barks to[47] go on and passed a Creek on the
South Side a bout 15 yards wide Coming out of an exten-
sive Prarie as the Creek has no name and this Day is the
4th of July we name this Independance[48] a Creek above this
Creek the wood Land is about 200 yards Back of those
wood is an extensive Praria open and High whigh may be
Seen Six or Seven [miles?] below ₐSaw₍ₐ₎ Grat~~e~~ number of
Goslins to day nearley Grown

the Last mentioned prarie I call Jo. Fieldes Snake prarie
Capt Lewis walked on Shore[49] we camped at one of the
Butifules Praries I ever Saw open and butifulley Divided
with Hills and ~~valleys~~ vallies all presenting them Selves
Thursday July ₍ₐ₎5th 1804₍ₐ₎ Set out errley this morning
Swam ouer Stray Horse a Cross the River to Join our
other Horses[50] prossed on for ₐtwo miles₍ₐ₎ under the
Banks of the old Kansas village formaley Stod in 1724
the co~~s~~ause of thes Indians moving from this place I cant
~~tell~~ Larn but natreley Concluded that war~~e~~ has reduced
thair nation and Compelled them to Rotir further in to
the Plaines with a view of Defending them Selves and

47. The snake is not identified but it apparently
was determined rather quickly that it was not
dangerous, even though Joseph Field's foot
swelled considerably. Moulton theorizes either
a slippery elm or Peruvian bark poultice was
applied. He thinks the Peruvian bark was most
likely used, since Lewis later used that as a
poultice. Whitehouse does not mention the
incident but does provide information about
the men's apparent practice of going barefoot
on the boat and along the shore. Perhaps Field
was barefoot when he was bitten. Whitehouse
notes that the day was very hot and when the
men stepped on the sand it was so hot it scalded
their feet and some men put on their moccasins.
(Moulton, 2:349 n; 11:34.)

48. Everyone notes naming the creek Independ-
ence in honor of the day and the country.
The bow gun was fired in the morning and
evening and an extra gill of whiskey was given
each man to celebrate the Fourth of July. The
other creek mentioned was christened Fourth
of July Creek. Neither creek has retained those
names, however. (Moulton, 2:348, 349 n.)

49. Floyd might have been copying from Clark's
entry for this day. There are many similarities
and some of the sentences are word for word
the same. His observation regarding the great
number of goslings through Lewis walking
on shore follows Clark's entry exactly. This
is not to say that Floyd might not have named
the prairie after Field—the men did sometimes
assign their own names to features (especially
Whitehouse)—but Floyd (as did Ordway)
rather consistently followed the names Clark
recorded. It is interesting to note how rarely
Floyd actually mentioned someone by name,
including Lewis and Clark. The other journalists more frequently mentioned names but still
did not commonly do so. (Moulton, 2:346.)

50. Apparently the party's new horse did not join
the others when sent ahead on 3 July. The
hunters who had them had apparently crossed
to the north (or east) side of the river. Whitehouse provides the location. (Moulton, 11:35.)

to operserve their enemey and to Defende them
selves on Horse Back encampt on the South
Side Friday July 6th 1804 Set out prosed under
a Jentell Breez from the South west the water
wase So trong that we could Hardley Steem
it, came 12 miles encampt
at the mouth of a Creek on the South Side of the
River 15 yards wide Saturday July 7th Set out
errley prosed along, passed Some Strong water
on the South Side, which compelled us to Draw
up by the Cord Clear morning verry warm Strong
water came 10 miles camt on the N. Side Sunday July 8th
Set out at Sun Rise Rain Last night with wind from the E.
passed Some good Land to day and High passed a Creek
on the N. Side it came in Back of a Island it is

a Bout 70 yards wide Colled Nadaway Creek
the Land is Good and well timberd camt on the
N. Side Monday July 9th 1804 Set out erley this
morning prosed on passed a Small Creek on the
South Side Colled monter creek High Land Rain to day Sailed
the gratist part of the day passed a prarie on the South Side whare Several
French famileys had Setled and made Corn Some years
ago Stayed two years
the Indians came Freckentley to See them and was verry
frendley passed a Creek on the South Side Colled Wolf Creek
it is about 60 yards wide the Land is good water Strong
made 10 miles Encamt on the South Side
Saw a fire on the N. Side thought it was Indians

to operserve their enemey and to Defende them Selves
on Horse Back[51] encamp[t] on the South Side Friday
July 6th 1804 Set out prossed under a Jentell Brees from
the South west the water wase So trong that we Could
Hardley ~~Steaun~~[?] ‸Steem[‸] it, ~~passed a Creek~~ Came
12 miles encamp[t] at the mouth of ‸a[‸] Creek on the South
Side of the River ‸Collo[d] Whipperwill Creek it is[‸]
15 yards wide[52] Saturday July 7th Set out errley prosed
along, passed Some Strong water on the South Side, which
Compelled us to Draw up by the Cord[53] Clear morning
verry warm Strong water Came 10 miles Camt on the
N. Side Sunday July 8th Set out at Sun Rise Rain Last
night with wind from the E. passed Some Good Land
to day ‸and[‸] High passed a Creek on the N. Side it
Cam in Back of Islad it is

a Bout 70 yards wide Colled Nadawa~~y~~ Creek the Land
is Good and well timber[d] Camt on the N. Side[54] Monday
July 9th 1804 Set out erley this morning prosed on
passed ~~a creek~~ a Small Creek on the South Side Colled
monter creek High Land Rain to day Sailed the Gratist
part of the day passed a prarie [‸]on the South Side[‸]
whare Seveal French fameleys had Setled and made Corn
~~a~~ Some Years ago ~~and Black Smith & Gun Smith~~ Stayed
two years the Indians came Freckentley to See them and
was verry frendley[55] passed a Creek on the South Side
Colled wolf Creek it is about 60 yards wide the Land is
Good water Strong made 10 miles encamt on the South
Side ~~the~~ Saw a fire on the N Side thougt it was ~~Indans~~

51. Floyd and Ordway almost certainly used Clark's
notes for this part of their entry. They read almost
the same and include what Clark wrote. Clark
references du Pratz's *History of Louisiana* (they
had the 1774 English translation with them)
in his account of the abandoned Kansa village.
Floyd makes no mention of several mishaps
that day moving the boat upstream. (Moulton,
2:348–51, 352 n; 9:20–21.)

52. Floyd makes more of the river's swiftness and
the party's difficulty in advancing against it than
the others. Both Clark and Ordway make note of
how heavily the men sweat, more "than I could
Suppose Could pass thro: the humane body,"
according to Clark. Both also relate that the creek
was named Whipperwhill Creek (Clark says
by him) due to a whippoorwill perching on the
boat. (Moulton, 2:352–53; 9:21.)

53. The phrase "which Compelled us to Draw up
by the Cord" is word for word the same as in
Clark's journal, even to the spelling and capital-
ization. (Moulton, 2:355.)

54. Clark notes that five men are sick with bad
headaches (most likely heat and sun related),
and several still suffer from boils. The captains
also issued detachment orders appointing new
cooks for each mess. The cook for Floyd's mess
was John B. Thompson. These "Superinten-
dants of Provision" were exempt from guard
and various other duties. Floyd made an attempt
to keep track of the substitutions for Thompson
in the guard rotation on the inside front cover
and a back page of his journal. (See the Appendix for these pages.) (Moulton, 2:357, 359–60.)

55. Clark notes that one of the French settlers was
their bowman, meaning either Pierre Cruzatte
or Francois Labiche (possibly the former given
later information about him living in the area).
Only Floyd mentions that friendly Indians frequently visited them. In entries for this date,
Gass is the only journalist to note that Joseph
Field is recovered from his snake bite. (Moulton,
2:362; 10:19.)

our flankien party sent over perogue over for them and when they got over saw no fire seposed it to be Indians fired our cannon for our men — **Tuesday July 10th** Set out when we could see, about us, when we came to the place it was our men which had left us two day ago much fateged had lay down and fell asleep passed a small creek on the South side called [illegible] Creek it comes through Bottom Land it is called after a man who by drawing his gun out of the Boat shot him self passed som strong water campt on the North side the Land is good **Wendesday July, 11th 1804.** Set out errley this morning prosed on passed a creek on the N° side called Tarcio Creek it comes in Back of a Id. on the N° side came to about 12 oclock P^m for the prosposs of resting on or two days the men is all sick encamt on an Id. on the Southe side floes in Creek called Gramma mohing Creek it is about 100 yards wide the Land is good and well timber High and well watered this Creek Runs up and Heds near the River platt — **Thursday July 12th** Som Hunters out on the N° side those on the South side not Return last night our object in Delaying hear is to take Same observations and rest the men who are much fatigued, armes and amunition Inspected all in good order — **Friday July 13th** Set out errley in the morrong

ouer flanken partey Sent ouer perogue over for them and
when they got over Saw no fire Seposed it to be Iindians
fired ouer Cannon for ouer men[56] Tuesday July 10th Set
out when we Could See, about us, ~~we~~ when we ~~ca~~ Came
to the place it was ouer men which had Left us two day a
go, ₍ₐ₎ much feteged had Lay down and fell aSleap₍ₐ₎ passed
a Є Small Creek on the South Side Colled ~~pac~~ pape Creek
it Comes through Bottom Land it is Called after a man
who by ~~draw~~ drawning his Gun out of the Boat Shot him
Self[57] passed Som Strong water Campt on the north Side
the Land is good Wenesday July, 11th 1804. Set out
errley this morning prosed on pasedd a Creek

on the N. Side Colled Tarcio Creek it Comes in Back of
a Is[d] on the N. Side ~~enc~~ Came to about 12 oclock P.m for
the porpos of resting on[e] or two day the men is all Sick
encamt on an IS[d] on the Southe Side floos in Creek Colled
Granna ~~maugh~~ mohug Creek[58] it is about 100 yards wide
the Land is good and well timber[d] High and well Waterd
this ~~Ri~~ Creek Runs ~~p~~ up and Heds near the River platt —
Thursday July 12th — Som Hunters out on the No. Side
those on the South Side not Return Last night ouer object
in Delaying hear is to take Some observations and rest
the men who are much fategeued, armes and amunition
enspected all in Good order — [59] Friday July 13th Set
out erley in the morning

56. Clark puts more significance on this event than
    Floyd or Ordway (Whitehouse and Gass make
    no mention of it). Ordway says gunfire rather
    than an actual fire, as Clark and Floyd do. Clark
    refers to their four flankers, meaning hunters.
    When they received no response to their signal,
    Indians were suspected. The bow gun was fired,
    not only to signal the flankers of their location
    but also to alert them to possible danger of what
    was believed might be a Sioux war party. The
    crew was prepared for action. The three journal-
    ists taking note of the event explain it was indeed
    their hunters in their 10 July entries. (Moulton,
    2:362–64; 9:22–23.)
57. Clark and Ordway identify him as a Spaniard
    but do not explain the accidental circumstances
    of him killing himself. Floyd had to have gotten
    such particulars from Cruzatte, Labiche, one of
    the French boatmen, or even possibly Dorion.
58. Although the spelling varies among the journal-
    ists, Floyd's spelling is sometimes difficult to
    even understand phonetically. This was the
    present Big Nemaha River, an Oto word mean-
    ing "miry water" whose name has been retained.
    It was much more than a creek. (Moulton,
    2:368 n.)
59. Floyd's 12 July entry is almost word for word
    the same as part of Clark's field notes entry. The
    sergeant must have copied it. The inspection
    was carried out in conjunction with the court
    martial of Alexander H. Willard for sleeping on
    guard duty. He was found guilty and sentenced
    to one hundred lashes on his bare back to be
    given in twenty-five lash increments over the
    next four evenings by the guard. (Moulton,
    2:368, 370–71.)

proced on our Jorney passed a Creek on the N. Side
Called the Big ~~Tar kula ha~~ River it is about 40 yads
wide and a verry mirey for horses to Cross the land is
Low a verry hard Storm Last night from the N. E. which Lasted for
about one ouer proceded with a small ~~rain~~ Souer of Rain
Wind fare Sailed all day Came 20½ miles Camt on a
a Sand Bare in the midel of the River a Small Shower
of Rain Saturday July 14th 1804 Set out at day Lite
Came one mild and ½ Came a Dredfulle hard Storme
~~the~~ from the South which Lasted for about one ouer and
half a which Coled us to jump out and hold hir She
Shipt about 2 Barrels of water Came one mile the
Wind fare Sailed passed a Creek on the N Side ~~Colled~~
Neshba Creek it is about 40 yards wide the Sand is Low
encamt on the South Side —

Sunday July 15th 1804 Set out at Six oclock
A M passed a Creek on the South Side Colled Plum
Run water verry Strong passed a Creek on the South Side
Colled We ma haw Creek the it is about 30 yards wide
the Land is High and godd encamt on the South Side

Monday July 16th we Set out verry early and
proceded on the Side of a Prarie the wind from the South
Sailed over Boat Run on a Sawyer Sailed all day made 20
miles passed Sevrall I Sd Camt on the North Side

Tuesday July 17th 1804 Lay by all this day
for to kill Some fresh meat Capt Lewis & Go Druger
went out hunting Drugher Killed 3 Deer the Land is

prosede on our Jorney passed a Creek on the N. Side Colled the Big ~ne ma har~ [^]Tar huo[^] River it is about 40 yads wide and ~is~ verry mirey for Horses to Cros the Land is Low a verry hard Storm Last night [^]from the N. E.[^] which Lasted for about one ouer proseded with a Small ~Rain~ Souer of Rain wind fare Sailed all day Came 20 ½ miles Camt on ~an~ a Sand Bare in the midel of the River a Small Shouer of Rain Saturday July 14ᵗʰ 1804 Set out ∧at[^] day Lite Came one mile and ½ Came a Dredfulle hard Storme ~the~ from the South which Lasted for about one ouer and half which Cosed us to Jump out and hold hir She Shipt about 2 Barrels of water[60] Came one miel the wind fare Sailed passed a Creek on the N Side Colled Neeshba Creek it is about 40 yards wide the Land is Low encamt on the Southe Side —

Sunday July 15ᵗʰ 1804 Set out at Six oclock Am pased a Creek on the Southe Side Colled Plumb Run water verry Strong passdd ∧a[^] Creek on the South Side Colled Nemahaw Creek ~the~ it is about 30 yards wide the Land is High and Good encamt on the Southe Side[61] monday July 16ᵗʰ we Set out verry early and prossed on the Side of a Prarie the wind from the South Sailed ouer Boat Run on a Sawyer[62] Sailed all day made 20 miles passed Sevrall ISᵈ Camt on the North Side Tuesday July 17ᵗʰ 1804 Lay by all this day for to kill som ~E~ fresh meat Capᵗ Lewis & Go. Druger went out Hunting[63] Drugher Killed 3 Deer the Land is

60. Clark gives a good account of the storm and yet another near disaster with the keelboat, but only Floyd mentions how much water the boat took on during the storm. Clark states the storm lasted forty minutes rather than Floyd's one and a half hours. (Moulton, 2:376–78.)

61. Clark and Ordway both note that Floyd and Drouillard went ashore that morning. In one of the few Lewis entries during the ascent of the lower Missouri, he discusses his discovery that his chronometer had stopped running. Ordway also mentions he went ashore with Clark, thus leaving only one sergeant (Nathaniel Pryor) on the boat (unless Floyd had returned by the time Ordway left). (Moulton, 2:380–81; 9:25.)

62. Floyd's mention of the boat being run on a sawyer sounds like another near disaster again understated by him. Apparently, though, while it could have been a disaster, the boat must have not been threatened because Clark and Ordway only mention it and Whitehouse and Gass do not mention it at all.

63. Ordway notes that they stayed in camp that day so the captains also could take some observations. Clark mentions the only reason being to take observations. Ordway mentions Lewis going out hunting but not with anyone else by name. It is not unusual that Lewis would go out with Drouillard. The latter had already proved his value to the expedition with his hunting and scouting skills and the captains had great confidence in him. If Lewis wanted to go hunting, especially in country that increasingly held more dangers and unknowns the farther upriver they went, Drouillard would be an excellent companion. (Moulton, 2:386, 388; 9:27.)

prarie Land the Blufs puts in about 2 miles from the
River and all prarie land between which Runs up and Down
for Som distance to from 20 to 30 miles ~~Thursda~~ Thursday, Wendesday July
18th 1804 we Set out at Sun Rise the day Clear wind fair
Sailed the Side of the prarie thear we toed for about 5 or 6 miles
the Elke Sine is erry plenty Deer is not as plenty as it
~~was~~ below passed Som High Clifts on the South Side
Which have the apperence of ~~iron~~ Iron ore
the Clay is Red passed a verry Strong pace of
Water Saw a Dog on the Bank which we Sepose
to be Indians had ben Lost this is the first Sine
of Indians we have Saw Campted on the South Side
the Land is Law that on the N. Side is prarie Land

Thursday July 19th we set out erly this morning

prosed on passed a Run on the South Side has no name
we ~~called Cherry~~ Cherry Run the land is high Clifes
and ~~bore~~ hore whare a Grate nomber of ~~these Grate Gr~~ Cherrees
thay Gro on Low Bushes about as High as a mans hed Came
9 miles past Several Isd. water Strong Campt on the
South Side on a Small willow Isd near the South Side
the land on the N. is Law. Land that on the Sou
is High prarie Land Friday July 20th

Set out at 6 oclock proseded on passed the mouth
of a Creek on the South Side Called Enys Creek it is about
35 yards wide it Camee in above Clifts oppset a willow
Isd. at this Clift thare is a fine Spring on the top of this
Hill is oppen prarie passed a Creek on the N. Side Called
Piggen Creek the land is Law ~~passed~~ that on the South
is High prarie land passed Several Bad Sand Bares
Campt ~~on~~ on the South Side under a large Hill W

prarie Land the Blufs puts in about 2 miles from the
River and all prarie Land betwen which Runs up and
Down for Som ˄distance ~~to~~ from[^] 20 to 30 miles
~~Thursda~~ Wendesday July 18th — 1804 ~~S~~ we Set out at
Sun Rise the day Clear wind fair Sailed the Side of the
Prarie Hear we toed for about 5 or 6 miles the Elke
Sine is erry plenty Deer is not as plenty as it was below
passed Som High Clifts on the South Side Which ~~a~~ hase
the apperence of ~~ore~~ Iron ore the Clay is Red passed
a verry Strong pace of water Saw a Dog on the Bank
which we Sepose to be Indians had ben Lost this is the
first Sine of Indians we have Saw[64] Camptd on the South
Side the Land is Low that on the N. Side is prarie Land
Thursday July 19th we Set out errly this morning

prosed on passed a Run on the South Side Has no name
we colled ~~Cherey~~ Cherry Run the Land is High Cliefes
and ~~bore~~ [^]pore[^] whare a Grate nomber of these ~~frute~~
~~Groe~~ [^]Cherres[^] thay Gro on Low ~~p~~ Bushes about as
High as as a mans hed[65] Came 9 miles past Several ISd
water Strong Campt on the South Side on a Small willow
ISd near the South Side the Land on the N. is Low Land
that on the South is High prarie Land Friday July 20th
Set out at 6. oclock proseded on passedt he mouth of
a Creek on the South Side colled Crys Creek it is about
35 yards wide it Comes in above Clifts oppset a willow
ISd at this Clift thare is a fine Spring on the top of this
Hill is oppen prarie passed a Creek on the N. Side colled
Piggen Creek[66] ~~is~~ the Land is Low ~~passed~~ that on the
South is High prarie Land passed Several Bad Sand Bares
Campt ~~one~~ on the South Side under a Large Hill

64. Floyd is the only one to mention that this dog
is the first recent sign of Indians they had seen
(other than the lost horses they had found).
Clark notes they gave it some meat, but it would
not come near them. (Moulton, 2:391–92; 9:27.)

65. Floyd is the only one to mention naming this
creek Cherry Run. He does not mention—as do
Ordway and Whitehouse—some of the cherries
they picked being put in one of the barrels
of whiskey. Clark's journal is of little use concerning the party's activities this day because
he spent most of the day walking on shore.
(Moulton, 9:27; 11:41.)

66. Pigeon Creek in Clark's field notes. (Moulton,
2:398.)

Saturday July 21th 1804 Set out at 4 oclock a m
prossed on over Journey Rain this morning wind fair
Sailed passed the mouth of the Grait River Plate on
the South Side it is much more Rapsuded than the
missorea it is about three quarters of a mile   from one mile to 3 mil
wide the Sand roles or out and formes a large Sand banes
in the middel of the missorea up the Plate it a-
bout one mile the stilles of Prarie Land about 2 days and
half up the Plate 2 nations of Indians Livee vic the
Souttoes the Ponney this River is not navigable for Boute to go up
it passed a Creek Colled the   on the South Side
it is about 20 yardes wide it Cames out of a Large Prarie
Campt on the South Side   Sunday July 22d Set out
verry erley this morning prossed on in Hopes to find Some

wood Land near the mouth of this Rifirst mentained River
bout Could not we prossed on about 10 miles at Lenth
found Sova on Both Sides of this River encampt on
the North Side   monday July 23d th 1804 we
Lay By fox the porpos of Resting and take Sour
observations at this place and to Send for Sour
Indians Sent George Drougher and over extif
Bows man wo is aquainted with the nations nothing
worth Relating to day   tuesday July 24th we mad
larg and Long Sage Staff and histed it up hested over
Collars in the morning for the Reseptione of
Indians who we expeckdt Hear when the Rain
and wind came So that we were forst to take

40

Saturday July 21ᵗʰ 1804 Set out at 4 oclock a m prosseded
on ouer Jouney Rain this morning wind fair Sailed passed
the mouth of the Grait River Plate on the South Side it is
much more Rappided than the missorea it is about ~~3 ½ ½~~
~~Three quarters of a mile~~ [^]from one mil to 3 miles[^] wide
the Sand Roles ~~or~~ out and formes ~~a~~ Large Sand bares in
the middel of the missorea up the Plate about one mile
the Hilles of Prarie Land a bout 2 days and half up the
Plate 2 nations of Indians Lives vic The Souttoes the
Ponney this River is not navigable for Boats to Go up it
passed ~~the~~ a Creek Colled the   on the South Side it
is about 20 yards wide it Comes out of a Large Prarie
Campt on the South Side⁶⁷ Sunday Jul 22ᵈ Set out~~e~~ verry
erley this morning prossed on in Hopes to find Some

wood Land near the mouth of this ~~Ri~~ first mentained
River bout Could not we prossed on about 10 miles at
Lenth found Som on Both Sides of the River encampt on
the North Side monday July 23ᵈᵗʰ 1804 we Lay By for the
porpos of Resting and take Som observations at this place
and to Send for Som Iindians⁶⁸ Sent George Drougher
and ouer ~~entarp~~ Bows man wo is aquainted with the
nations⁶⁹ nothing worth Relating to day tuesday July 24ᵗʰ
we mad Larg. and Long f[l]age Staff and Histed it up
Histed ouer Collars [colors] in the morning⁷⁰ ~~wh~~ for the
Reseptions of Indians who we expecedt Hear when the
Rain and wind Came So that we wase forst to take

67. Similar in many respects to other journalists,
although not as long or detailed (as usual) as
Clark's or Ordway's journal entries. Floyd's
crossed-out three-quarters of a mile refers to the
Platte's width at its mouth and the one to three
miles to its varying width upstream. This information came from either Labiche or Cruzatte.
Both were half French and half Omaha Indian
and were familiar with the area, especially
Cruzatte. Clark and Ordway state they got the
information from the French bowman. Only
Gass gives an approximate translation of the
French *platte*, calling it Shallow River rather
than the more accurate flat. The Indian tribes
are the previously mentioned Oto and Pawnee.
The name of the creek he leaves blank is Papil-
lion or Butterfly Creek. The creek still bears
its French name today. Lewis and Clark with
six men took one of the pirogues a mile up the
Platte, but it is not stated who comprised the
party. The Platte might not have been suitable
for river traffic, but it became famous as the
watercourse along which roads—wagon and
rail—would stretch westward across the plains.
The Astorians established an overland route
along the Platte less than a decade after Lewis
and Clark. With the establishment of the Oregon/
Mormon/California Trails in the 1840s and the
Union Pacific Railroad in the 1860s, the Platte
River valley served as a major avenue of transportation and westward expansion. (Moulton,
2:401–4; 10:22.)

68. This was White Catfish Camp as called in
Clark's and Whitehouse's journals. It apparently
was christened that because there Silas Good-
rich caught a white catfish (possibly a channel
catfish—a new species to them) on 23 July. In
addition to waiting for Drouillard and Cruzatte
to return with a hoped-for Indian delegation
of Otos and Pawnees, Lewis and Clark also delayed here working on reports and maps, respectively. The plan was to send someone back down
the river from the mouth of the Platte with the
reports and Clark's map of the Missouri with
related table of distances, and so on. No one
from the party is known to have gone back. It
would be spring 1805 before these reports and
maps, as well as other material, returned down-
river. (Moulton, 2:416, 418; 11:44.)

69. Drouillard and Cruzatte. As previously mentioned, Cruzatte was familiar with the area
and its tribes and was likely the bowman who
had spent two winters on the Platte, probably
with Indians or as their neighbor. (Moulton,
2:415–16.)

70. Floyd seems to indicate that the flagpole was
made and the flag hoisted on that day. If so, he
is in error because that had been done the previous day. It may be that he is just vague in the
way he notes it, since he says that they hoisted
their colors in the morning after just writing
that they made the staff and hoisted the flag.
(Moulton, 2:415; 9:29; 11:44.)

it down sent ~~on~~ some of our men ouit to Hunt
some over timber for to make some ores as the
timber of that cind is verry Large up the River
Continued Shouery all day Wendesday July 25th
Continued hear as the Cafty is not Don ther Riting our
men Returnd whome we had sint to the town and
found non of them at home but seed some fresh
sine of them ~~Thursday July 27th we set~~
~~out at 11 oclock P. m progsed on under a sentil Brees~~
~~from the S. E. sied~~ Thursday July 26th our.
men fineshed the oars nothing worth Relating except
the wind was verry villant from the South Egt

Friday July 27th Swam our Horses over ~~11~~ on to the
South Side on acount of the travilen ie beter
Set out at 12 oclock P. m progsed on under a sentell
Brees from the South Egte Sailed made 10 miles
enenut on the South side at Prarie

Satturday July 28th Set out verry erley this
morning progsed on passed a Creek on the ~~S~~
North Side Colled Beaver Creek is about 20 yards wide
the sand is Low that on the South is Prarie Land
Rain the fore part of the day the Latter part Clear
with wind from the North Egt. made 10 miles
Campt on the N. Side the sand is Low that on the
South is High Prarie Land our flanker partey
Came with one Indian thay found on the South side

it down Sent ~~on~~ Some of ouer men out ˄to[˄] Hunt Some
ore timber for to make Some ores as the timber of that
Coind is verry Carse [scarce] up the River[71] Continued
Shouery all day Wendesday July 25th Continued Hear
as the Capts is not Don there Riting ouer men Returnd
whome we had Sent to the town and found non of them
at Home but Seen Some fresh Sine of them ~~Thuresday~~
~~July 27th we Set out at 12 oclock P.m prossed on under~~
~~a Jentil Brees from the S. E. Sited~~ Thursday July 26th
ouer men fineshed the oares nothing worthe Relating
except the wind was verry villant from the South Est

Friday July 27th Swam ouer Horses over ~~th~~ on to the
South Side on acount of the travilen is beter[72] Set out at
12 oclock P.m prossed on under a Jentell Brees from the
South Este Sailed made 10 miles encmt on the South Side
at Prarie   Saturday July 28th Set out verry erley this
morning prossed on passed a Creek on the ~~South~~ North
Side Colled Beaver Creek[73] is about 20 yards wide the
Land is Low that on the South is Prarie Land Rain the
fore part of the day the Latter part Clear with wind from
the North Est made 10 miles Campt on the N. Side the
Land is Low that on the South is High prarie Land ouer
flanken partey Came with one Indian thay found on the
South Side[74]

71. Floyd is the only one to mention that the reason
they were apparently making oars at this time
was due to the scarcity of proper timber (ash
was preferred) for them farther upstream as they
edged closer to the Great Plains and away from
the woodlands and transitional country they
had been passing through. Only Clark mentions
that they were also making poles for the boats.
(Moulton, 2:421.)

72. Floyd is the only one to comment that the horses
were swum across to the south side of the river
because the traveling was easier. Clark writes
that it was because the hunters were going to
travel and hunt on that side of the river (perhaps
because traveling was easier). (Moulton, 2:421.)

73. Only Floyd calls it Beaver Creek. No beaver
are mentioned as being seen in the journals for
this day, but perhaps he saw one or some sign
of beaver. Clark calls the stream Indian Knob
Creek, while Whitehouse, Ordway, and Gass all
call it Round Knob Creek. It probably is present
Pigeon Creek in Pottawattamie County, Iowa.
(Moulton, 2:423–24, 425 n; 9:30; 10:23; 11:47.)

74. Drouillard was one member of the flanking—
or hunting—party. Gass writes that two of their
men came with an Indian. Ordway and Whitehouse say Drouillard did; and in his field notes
Clark says the flanking party came in with a
Missouria Indian but revised it to Drouillard
bringing the Indian in when he wrote his fair
copy. There are also contradictions regarding
the Indian's tribal affiliation. Only Clark says
he was a Missouria. Ordway, Whitehouse, and
Gass all identify him as an Oto. Given the close
association of the tribes, it could be that the
enlisted men simply identified the Indian by
the dominant tribe, whereas Clark was more
specific in ascertaining his tribal affiliation.
(Moulton, 2:423–24; 9:30–31; 10:23; 11:46.)

Sunday July 29th we set out after we Dispashed
the Indian and one [strikethrough] of ouer men [strikethrough] with him
to bring the Rest of his party the Reason this man
gives of his being with So Small a party is that he
has not got horses to go in the Large pravries after the
Bufflows but stayes about the Town and River to hunte
the Elke to beporte his have familys passed the mauth
of Boyers River on the N. Side it about 30 yards wide
the Land is Low Bottom Land out from the River
is High hills Campt on the North Side at a pravie
monday July 30th Set out verry erley this morning
Cam 3 miles Sopt for the man whome we had
Sent with the Indian yesterday He has not Returnd
yet [strikethrough] Sent 2 men out Hunting Did not Return

Last night Campt on the South Side at pravie
Tuesday July 31 1804 we Lay By for
to See the Indianes who we expect hear to See the
Captaynes, I am verry Sick and has ben for Som time
but have Recoverd my helth again the Indianes have not
Came yet this place is Called Council Bluff the
2 men went out on the 30th of July and Lost ouer
horses Wensday august 1 1804 Lay by
all this Day expecting the Indianes every ouer
Sent George Drougher out to Hunt ouer Horses
Sent one man Down the River to whare
we eat Diner on the 28th of July to See if ouy
Indianes ware had been thare He Returnd
and saw no Syen of them

Sunday July 29ᵗʰ we Set out after we Dspashed the Indian
and one m̶ of ouer men t̶h̶a̶t̶ with him to bring the Rest
of his party[75] the Reasen this man Gives of His being
with t̶h̶ So Small a party is that He S̶t̶ Has not Got Horses
to Go in the Large praries after the Buflows but Stayes
about the Town and River to Hunte the Elke to Seporte
H̶i̶s̶ ₐthare₍ₐ₎ famileys[76] passed the mouth of Boyers River
on the N. Side it about 30 yards wide the Land is Low
Bottom Land out from the River is High Hills Campᵗ
on the North Side at a prarie monday July 30ᵗʰ Set out
verry erley this morning Cam 3 miles Sopt for the man
whome we Had Sent with the Indian yesterday He has
not Returnd yet C̶a̶m̶p̶t̶ Sent 2 men out Hunting Did
not Return

Last night[77] Tuesday July 31th 1804 ₐCampt on the South
Side at prarie₍ₐ₎ we Lay By for to See the Indaines who
we expect Hear to See u̶s̶ the Captains,[78] I am verry Sick
and Has ben for Somtime but have Recoverd my helth
again[79] The Indianes have not Come yet this place is
Colled Council Bluff t̶h̶e̶ 2 men went out on the 30ᵗʰ of
July and Lost ouer horses[80] Wendesday august 1th 1804
Lay by all this day expecting the Indianess every ouer
Sent George Draugher out to Hunt ouer Horses Sent
one man Down the River to whare we eat Diner on the
28ᵗʰ of July to See if aney Indianes w̶a̶r̶e̶ Had been thare
He Returnd and Saw no Sigen of them[81]

75. The man sent with the Oto/Missouria Indian
was La Liberté, one of the French-Canadian
engagés. Moulton discusses the confusion surrounding his name and who he might have
been. Taking into account the French custom
of nicknames—or *dit* names—might identify
him as Joseph Collin, who appears on the
engagé list. Ordway states that he was sent because he could speak the Oto language. As
Floyd and the others report, he left the expedition (not actually deserting because he had been
hired, not enlisted) at this time and was never
seen again except by the party sent after him,
which he eluded. (Moulton, 2:526–28; 9:31.)

76. Floyd is the only one to report this information.
Because he did not speak Oto, he must have
heard it by listening to the conversation the captains had with their Indian visitor or by talking
with those involved in the meeting. Clark reports similar information but not about his band
having no horses and therefore being compelled
to stay near the river to hunt elk to support their
families. (Moulton, 2:423–24.)

77. There were interesting occurrences on 30 July
that Floyd does not mention. On this date in
his journal, Clark notes that Floyd was "verry
unwell a bad Cold &c." This is the first mention
of Floyd being sick—perhaps with the malady
that would eventually kill him three weeks later.
He may be one of those men included in the
unnamed group of sick that Clark mentioned
earlier. It also might explain why Floyd's journal
entries had been rather brief and stated only the
basic facts in recent days. Although indications
are that his earlier malady might have been related to his hand, is it possible that the apparent
illness or injury that struck Floyd in late June
was related to the one that struck him in late
July? (Moulton, 2:429.)

78. Floyd's insertion mark indicates 31 July is the
intended place for the location of their camp,
not at the end of the 30 July entry. His revision
from the expected arrival of the Indians to see
"us" to "the Captains" is interesting and perhaps provides an insight into the perspective the
enlisted men had regarding the Corps' Indian
mission and the role they played—or didn't play.

79. As discussed in the Introduction, 31 July was
Floyd's first mention of having been sick. Ordway mentions it the same day in his journal.
One wonders if Floyd and Ordway would have
mentioned it at all if Clark had not. This could
be an example of their reticence to mention it
until their captain did or their copying from
Clark and each other and consequently men-
tioning it due to that. Ordway does put a length
to the illness, stating it was several days. Floyd,
writing he had been ill for some time, would
indicate longer than a few days. Either he was
being vague (not unusual in his and the other
enlisted men's journals) or he knew he had been
sick longer than anyone else knew. Writing that
"I am verry Sick" would indicate that he has not
recovered, but then he contradicts himself by
writing that "[I] have Recoverd my helth again."

(continued on page 83)

Thursday august 2ᵈ over men have
bought we had sent after our Horses Returnd
with them and **killed** one Elke the Indian
over men killed 3 Deer to day the Indianes came whou
we had expected thay fired meney guings when thay
came in site of us and we ansered them with the
Cannon thay came in about 2 hundred yardes of us
Capt Lewis and Clark met them at Shakering
Handes we fired another Cannon thare
wase **6** Chiefs and 7 men and one Firench man
with them who has lived with them for som
yeares and has a familey with them —

Friday august 3ᵈ the Council was held
and all partes was agreed the Captens give then
meney presentes they is the ottoe and the
Missouriees the Mizeouries is a verry small
nathion the ottoes is a verry large nathion
So thay live in one village on the Plate
River after the Council was over we took our
leave of them and embarked at 3. oclock P m
under a gentell Brees from the south Est
Sailed made 6 miles Campt on the south side the land
low, that on the N. prarie land —
— Satturday august 4ᵗʰ 1804 Set out evry this
morning after the Rain was over it Rained last night
with wind and thunder from the N. w. it losted about

Thursday auguste 2^dth ouer men ~~how~~ hough we had
Sent ~~to~~ after ouer Horses Return^d with them[82] and Killed
one Elke ~~the Indian~~ ouer men Killed 3 Deer to day the
Indianes Came whare we had expected thay fired meney
Gunes when thay Came in Site of us and we ansered them
withe the Cannon thay Came in about 2 hundred yardes
of us Capt Lewis and Clark met them at Shakeing Handes
we fired another Cannon – thare was ~~Six~~ 6 Chiefs and
7 men and one French man with them who has Lived with
them for som yeares and has a familey with them —[83]

Friday ~~1~~ august 3^dth the Council was held and all partes
was agreed the Captens Give then meney presentes thes
is the ottoe and the Missouries the Missouries is a verry
Small nathion the ottoes is a verry Large nathion So thay
Live in one village on the Plate River after the Council
was over ‸we‿ took ouer Leave of them and embarked
at 3 oclock P.m under a Jentell Brees from the South Es^t
Sailed made 6 miles Campt on the South Side the Land
Low, that on the N. prarie Land — S

Satturday august 4th 1804 Set out erry this ‸morning‿
after the Rain was over it Rained Last night with wind
and thunder ‸from the‿ N. w. it Lasted about

(continued from page 81)

Perhaps this was a slip of tense, using "am" instead of "was." The day before, Clark reported
that Floyd was "verry unwell," while this day
Ordway wrote that Floyd was "Gitting Some
better." It seems unlikely that he would be
entirely well the next day. Perhaps he was im-
proving but still not fully recovered (and never
would be). Did the young sergeant think it un-
military to comment on personal matters? or to
complain about being sick or suffering personal
discomfort? (Moulton, 2:429; 9:33.)

80. Lewis names the area Council Bluffs in his
31 July observations. Otherwise, Floyd is the
only person to record the name the captains
gave to the area this early. Clark provides a
good description of the countryside and events
in camp while waiting for the Indians to arrive,
but he does not state the name Council Bluff
until 3 August. Gass and Whitehouse identify
it by that name on 2 August and Ordway on
3 August. The Field brothers lost the horses,
which were recovered on 2 August by Drouillard
and John Colter. This is an example of Floyd's—
and other journalists'—frequent practice (we
could say even failure) to not use names. Given
the close relationship between Floyd and the
two brothers—from Kentucky, serving in the
same squad together—one would think that he
would use their names. Almost the only name
Floyd does use, as do some of the other journalists, is Drouillard. Floyd's 1 August entry is an
example. Clark softens the accusation that the
Field brothers lost the horses recorded in his
field notes by revising his fair copy journal
entry to read that the horses had strayed off and
not assigning blame to the brothers. (Moulton,
2:428–40; 9:34; 10:25; 11:49.)

81. The man was George Gibson, one of the "Young
Kentuckians," and again someone Floyd knew
well. One would think that Floyd would be in-
clined to name him, but that is clearly not his
style. The other journalists are better regarding
assigning names to the participants in the various
expedition events, but they frequently do not
either. Only Whitehouse identifies Gibson by
name concerning this event. Even Clark simply
writes that one more man was sent back to
check the old camp. (Moulton, 2:433–34; 11:49.)

82. The two men were Drouillard and Colter, as
previously mentioned. Clark elaborates in his
fair copy journal to name Colter; he does not
in his field notes. He states that they found the
horses twelve miles south of camp. Colter was
one of the Kentuckians. He was an excellent
hunter and is one of the few enlisted members
of the Corps for which there is a physical description: 5 foot 10 inches tall with blue eyes,
somewhat shy, and with a quick mind. He was

(continued on page 85)

an over prossed on the morning Clear passed
a Creek on the South Side Called as it has no
name and the Council was Held be low it about 7 miles we
call it Council Creek or Board this Creek Comes out
of a Large Pond which Lays Under the High prarie
Hills the wood Sand is not plenty hear ordley
along the River Banks in places, passed som bad
Sand bars enamt on the South Side a Large prarie
that on the N. is prarie Land Sunday August 5 th
Set out erley this morning Cam 2 miles when a verry
hard Storm of wind and Rain from the North West it
it Lasted about 2 ouers and Cleard up I have Remarked that
I have not heard much thunder in this Countrey Lightining is
Common as in other Countreys a verry Large Snake was Killed
to day Called the Bull Snake his Colure Somthing Like

a Rattel Snake passed Severall Bad Sand bars made
16 miles Campt on the North Side at Som wood Lord that
on the South is woodland monday August 6 th 1804
we Set out at erley ouer this morning prossed on passed
a Creek on the N. Side Called Soldiers Creek it Comes
in Back of a field near the N. S. about 12 oClock Last
night a villant Storm of wind and Rain from the N. W—
Camt on the South Side the Land Low that on
the N S. the Sain Tuesday August 7 th
Set out at 6 oclock A.m prossed on day Clear wind
from the north west — on the 4 th of this month one of
oues men by the name of Moses. B. Reede went Back to oues
Camp whare we had Left in the morning, to Git his
Knife which he Had Left at the Camp bout the Boat
went on and He Did not Return, for that night

an ouer prossed on the morning Clear passed a Creek on
the South Side Colled as it has no name and the Council
was Held be low it about 7 miles we Call it Council Creek
or Pond[84] this Creek Comes out of a Large Pond which
Lays under the High praries Hills the wood Land is
not plenty hear ondley along the River Banks in places,
passed Som bad Sand bares en[c]amt on the South Side
a Large prarie that on the N. is prarie Land Sunday
august 5th Set out erley this morning Cam 2 miles when
a verry hard Storm of wind fr and Rain from the North
west [^]Est[^] it Lasted about 2 ouers ˄and[^] Cleard up I
have Remarked that I have not heard much thunder in this
Countrey Lightining is Common as in other Countreys
a verry Large Snake was Killed to day Colled the Bull
Snake his Colure Somthing Like

a Rattel Snake[85] passed Severrall Bad Sand bares made
16 miles Campt on the North Side at Som wood Land
that on the South is woo[d] Land moneday August 6th
1804 we Set out at a erley ouer this morning prossed on
passed a Creek on the N. Side Colled Soldiers Creek it
Comes in Back of a Isld near the N. S. about 12 oclock
Last night a villant ˄Storm of[^] Rwind and Rain from the
N. W — Camt on the South Side the Land Low that on
the N S. the Saim Tuesday August 7th Set out at 6 oclock
A.m prossed on day Clear wind from the North west –
on the 4th of this month one of ouer men by the name of
Moses B. Reed went Back to ouer Campt whare we had
Left in the morning, to Git his Knife which he Had Left at
the Camp boat the Boat went on and He Did not Return,
pon e that night

(continued from page 83)

so enamored of the West that he received
permission from the captains at the Mandan-
Hidatsa villages in August 1806 to return westward. He remained in the West for four years,
becoming a legend for his exploits and adventures and earning the sobriquet "First of the
Mountain Men." He settled in Missouri in the
neighborhood of Charette in 1810 after deciding
his luck was used up. He and Drouillard were
sometimes paired together hunting. Both were
on the same trapping venture in 1810 on which
Drouillard was killed by Blackfeet. (Moulton,
2:435–36; 11:49; Yater, p. 9.)

83. Floyd offers one of the better accounts of the
arrival of the Oto and the Missouria, being more
specific than the other journalists. The Oto
lived in one village on the lower Platte near the
mouth of the Elkhorn River. Over the course
of the late seventeenth and the eighteenth cen-
turies they had drifted from the Mississippi
River across Iowa, living with their relatives
the Iowa, until establishing their village on the
lower Platte by the late 1700s. The addition of
the Missouria in the 1790s boosted their numbers, but they still remained a small tribe. The
Frenchman was one Faufong or Fairfong, as
well as other variations of the spelling of his
name in the journals. He apparently lived as
a trader among the Oto but he has never been
fully identified. Clark noted the location of
Council Bluff as a good site for a trading post
and Fort Atkinson was established there in 1819.
For a more detailed account of the Corps' first
Indian council and all other Indian relations on
the expedition see James Ronda's *Lewis and
Clark among the Indians*. (Moulton, 2:435–36,
437 n, 440, 443 n; 9:33; 10:25; 11:49–50.)

84. Floyd is the only one to name the creek either
Council or Pond. Clark comes closest, listing
it in his course and distance notes as Creek of
the Ponds. Moulton identifies it as probably
being Fish Creek at Blair, Washington County,
Nebraska. Floyd does not mention several things
noted by the others. His focus on the watercourses and countryside is a constant in his
journal. One wonders if it might indicate his
duties for that day on the keelboat, particularly
at the bow or helm, given his focus on these
two areas to the exclusion of reporting on other
events. (Moulton, 2:444, 446 n.)

85. Floyd's comments on the thunder and lightning
and the snake are word for word the same as
Clark wrote in his field notes. In fact, in his field
notes, Clark crossed out the statement about
lightning being common. Since he revised this
statement in his fair copy it might be possible
that he decided this statement was inaccurate
and therefore crossed it out when preparing

(continued on page 87)

nor the next day nor night, pon examining his map —
Sack we found that he had taken his Cloas and all
His powder and Balles, and had hid them out
that night and had made that an excuse to Desarte
from us with out aney Just Case we never minded
the Said man untill the 7th we sent 4 men after
him we expect he will make for the ottoe town
as it is not mor than 2 days Jorney from whare he
Runaway from us made 16 miles Water Good made 16
miles Camped on the North Sid at Some wood Land

Wensday Augt 8th 1804 Set out this morning at the usele tim
Day Clear wind from the N.W. proceed on passed the mouth
of the Littel Sieu River on the N. Side it is about 80 yards wide
this River is navigable for Boats to go up for Som distance in
the Cuntrey and Runes parelel with the Missourie
2 miles above on a sand Bare Saw Grait Number of Pelicans
Capt Clark went out on the South Side and J. Collines Killed an Elke water Bad
made 12 miles Camp on the N. Side the Land is Low marchey
Land that on the South is prarie Land Thursday augt
the 9th Set out at 7. oclock a.m. after the fague was gon which is verry
thick in this Cuntrey Capt Clark and my Self went out
on the South side passed a verry Bad place in the River
whare the water is verry shellow and 17 miles
Camped on the South Side at prarie

Set out far erely over this morning

Friday augt the 10th Set out erely over this
morning proceed on passed a bad sand bare which is verry
shellow made 23 miles Camped on a sand bare on the

nor the next day nor Night, pon examining his nap-Sack
we found that he had taken his ~~Col~~ Cloas and all His powder and Balles, and had ~~E~~ hid them out that night and had
made that an excuse to Desarte from us with out aney Jest
Case ~~we~~ never minded the Said man utill the 7ᵗʰ ~~the~~ we
Sent 4 men after him we expect he will make for the ottoe
town as it is not mor than 2 days Jorney from whare he
Run away from us⁸⁶ ~~made 16 miles~~ Water Good made
16 miles Campᵈ on the ~~South~~ North Sid at Some wood
Land [^]Wenesday[^] Augᵗ 8ᵗʰ 1804 Set out this morning
at the usele time day Clear wind from the N. W. prossed
on passed the mouth of the Littel Sᵗoue River on the
N. Side it is about 80 yaᵈs wide this River is navigable
for Boates to Go upit for Som Distance in the Cuntrey
and Runes parelel with the Missourie

2 miles above on a Sand Bare Saw Grait ~~qu~~ Nomber
of Pelicans Capᵗ Clark went out on the South Side a
~~and Jo Colline~~ and ~~one man the~~ Jo Collines Killed on
Elke water Bad⁸⁷ mad 12 miles Campᵈ on the N. Side
the Land is Low march Land that on the South is prarie
Land Thursday augt the 9ᵗʰ Set out at 7 oclock a m
~~we could see about us the~~ after the fague was Gon which
~~was~~ [^]is[^] verry thick in this Cuntrey Capᵗ Clark and
my Self went out on the South side passed a verry Bad
place in the River whare the water is verry Shellow mad
17 miles Campᵈ on the South Side at prarie⁸⁸
~~Set out at errley ouer this morning~~
Friday augt the 10ᵗʰ Set out at errley ouer this morning
prosed on passed abad Sand bare which is verry Shallow
made 23 miles Camped on a band [sand] bare on the

(continued from page 85)

his fair copy. Floyd had actually previously
commented seven times on thunder accompanying storms but had not mentioned lightning, so
he contradicts himself in copying what Clark
wrote. Lewis writes a description of the snake.
Floyd mentions nothing of several other events
that day. (Moulton, 2:447-50.)

86. Floyd provides the best details concerning Moses
Reed's desertion. Clark, Ordway, and Gass had
all noted Reed's absence on 4 August, and Whitehouse noted it on 5 August—actually already stating then that he had deserted. Ordway and Clark
mention him again on 6 August, stating they have
every reason to believe that he had deserted. This
must be when Reed's deception, that Floyd de-
scribes, was discovered. Both also mention La
Liberté and his absence, stating the belief that he
got lost trying to join them at Council Bluff. Clark
goes on to say that a four-man party is going to be
sent out to look for both men. Floyd makes clear
that Reed has no "Jest Case" to do such a thing.
The four men sent after Reed, as well as La Liberté, were Drouillard (of course!), Reubin Field,
William Bratton, and Labiche. Clark, Gass, and
Ordway all mention that the party had orders
to bring Reed in "Dead or alive." Clark explains
that they had orders to kill Reed if he would not
"give up Peaceibly." They were to catch up with
the party at the Omaha Indian village, where it
would wait for them. (Moulton, 2:452-56; 9:34-35;
10:25-26; 11:52.)

87. Everyone commented on the pelicans. Only Floyd
does not mention Lewis killing one and their ex-
periment of filling its mouth pouch with five gal-
lons of water. Lewis gives a thorough description
of the American white pelican, a bird that was
known in the East at that time. It had actually been
observed at Camp Dubois that spring but not in
the numbers the Corps observed them now. The
other journalists reported that they numbered in
the hundreds, with the exception of Whitehouse,
who recorded their number at five thousand to six
thousand. Clark, Ordway, and Gass comment on
the former's hunting excursion with John Collins.
Clark and Ordway make it clear that Collins killed
the elk. Clark had brought a small caliber gun
with him, perhaps his fusil (or fuzee), with which
he wounded but apparently failed to kill an elk
because of the gun's small caliber. Collins (not
to be confused with engagé Joseph Collin—also
known as La Liberté) had apparently begun to re-
deem himself in the eyes of the captains, or at least
Clark, since his 29 June court martial. Collins is
believed to have engaged in the fur trade on the
Missouri and been killed in a fight with the Arikaras
in 1823. Floyd's "bad water" notes another difficult
stretch of the Missouri in which the Corps encountered a number of bends and a great many sand
bars and snags. (Moulton, 2:329, 457-63, 515; 9:36;
10:26; 11:52-53.)

(continued on page 89)

N. Side the Land on the S.S. is High Hilley Land

Satturday august 11th 1804 Set out after a verry
hard Storm this morning of wind and Rain Continued
untill 9 oclock A m. Cleard up proged on passed
a high Bluff whare the Kinge of the Mahas Died
about 4 yeares ago the Hill on which he is berried
is about 300 feet High the nation goes 2 or 3 times
a year to Cryes over him Captn Lewis and Clark
went up on the Hill to see the grave thay histed
a flage on his grave ve nener for him which well
pleas the indiones, passed the mouth of a Creek
on the South Side Colled Waic Con Di Pecche
or the Grait Sperite Bad this Chief and
ware this Chief died about 300 Hundred of his
men with the small pox this Chief name was

the Black Bird made 15 miles Camped on the
North Side Sunday august 12th 1804 Set out at
the usel time proged on under a Gentel Breed from
North Est Sailed day Clear passed Red Seeder Bluff on the South
Side made 16 miles Camped on a Sand bare in the middel of the River

Monday august 13th Set out verry erley this morning
proged on under a Gentel Breed from the South Est
Sailed morning Clouday about 10. o:k, it Cleared up
we Rived at the Mahas village about 2 oclock P m
Sent Som of auer men to se if aney of the natives
was at Home thay Returnd found none of Them at Home

Tuesday August 14th Lay by for auer men How we
had Sent after the Deserter on the 7th they Indians
only live at this village has not Live at the town Sence
the Smalepox was so bad abut 4 years ago thay Burnt thave

N. Side the Land on the S. S. is High Hilley Land Satturday august 11ᵗʰ 1804 Set out after a verry hard Storm this
morning of wind and Rain continued untill 9 oclock A m.
and Cleard up prosed on passed a high Bluff whare the
Kinge of the Mahas Died about 4 yeares ago the Hill on
which he is berred is about 300 feet High the nathion
Goes 2 or 3 times a yeare to Cryes over him Capᵗ Lewis
and Clark went up on the Hill to See ~~him~~ [^]the Grave[^]
thay histed a flage on his Grave as ~~present~~ [^]noner[^]
[honor] for him which will pleas the Indianes, passed
the mouth of a Creek on the South Side Colled Waie Con
Di Peeche ˄or the Grait Sperit is Bad[^] ware this Chief
~~Didd~~ died ˄and[^] about 300 Hundred of his men with
the Small pox this Chiefs name was

the Black Bird⁸⁹ ~~Cam~~ made 15 miles Campeᵈ on the
North Side Sunday august 12ᵗʰ 1804 Set out at the usel
time prosed on under a Jentel Brees from North Esᵗ
Sailed day Clear passed Red Seeder Bluffs on the South
Side ~~this the first Seeder we have Seen Sence we Left the~~
~~S~~ made 16 miles Camped on a Sand bare in the middel of
the River⁹⁰ monday august 13ᵗʰ Set out verry erley this
morning prosed on under a Jentel Brees from the South
Esᵗ – Sailed ~~day Cou~~ morning Clouday about 10. o.ck.
it Cleared up we aRived at the Mahas village about
2 oclock P.m Sent Som of ouer men to Se if aney of the
natives was at Home thay Returnd found none of them
at Home⁹¹ Tuesday august 14ᵗʰ Lay by for ouer men
How [who] we had Sent after the Desarter on the 7ᵗʰ thes
Indians ~~onley live at this village~~ has not Live at the town
Sence the Smallpoks was So bad abut 4 years ago thay
Burnt thare

(continued from page 87)

88. All the journalists mention the fog but only
Whitehouse has the party camping on the north-
ern bank that night. It almost certainly was the
south (or west) side of the river as the others
note. Clark and Floyd hunting on the south side
is further evidence of the boats putting to on that
side. Only Ordway names Floyd as accompanying Clark. Even Clark does not mention Floyd
being with him. Clark killed a turkey, Floyd
nothing. The "verry bad place in the River"
might have been where the Missouri had recently cut through a bend, trimming a reported
fifteen miles from the old route and thus their
trip. (Moulton, 2:464; 9:36–37; 10:27; 11:53.)

89. It is believed that Draper did this red underlining (see note 17). This stop at the Omaha chief
Blackbird's grave is the main feature of all the
entries that day. The amount of information varies but is consistent. Several mention the flag
hoisted being white, but only Clark comments
that it was bound with red, blue, and white.
Floyd uses the same translated name for Great
Spirit is Bad Creek as Clark. Floyd repeats "the
Grait Sperit is Bad" in the left margin of his
journal. Both hill and creek are known today as
Blackbird Hill and Blackbird Creek, Thurston
County, Nebraska. Blackbird was indeed a king
among his people and was also believed to be
a sorcerer. This and the deadly smallpox experienced by the Omahas in their village there
might explain the Indian name for the creek.
(Moulton, 2:469–70; 9:37; 10:27; 11:54.)

90. Floyd makes no mention of Peter Wiser (Weiser)
replacing John Thompson as the cook and superintendent of provisions in his squad. Thompson
apparently was not doing his job or was needed
for other duties. This appointment might reflect
a shifting in the make-up of the squads since
Weiser served in Sergeant Pryor's squad per
the 26 May detachment orders. Floyd might
have believed it inappropriate or inconsequen-
tial to say anything. Or perhaps he was declin-
ing toward his final illness and only stating the
main facts of the day's events. (Moulton, 2:255,
359–60, 472–74.)

91. The Omahas were believed to still be out on the
plains hunting buffalo. In his entry for the next
day, however, Floyd explains how the Omahas
have been affected by the smallpox and when
they are actually in their village. Clark provides
a good description of these two days, as does
Ordway, who led the advance party to the village.
The Omahas had once been a powerful tribe,
to be feared by other tribes, but the smallpox
that devastated them in 1799–1800 broke their
strength. Their neighbors farther north, like the
Teton Sioux and the Arikaras, now dominated
them and Missouri River trade. (Moulton,
2:478–79, 482 n; 9:38–39.)

town and onley live about it in the winter and in the
Spring Go all of them in the prarie after the Bufflow and
dos not Return untill the fall to meet the French traders thay Rase
no Corn nor aney thing excep som times thay Rase som Corn
and then the Ottoe nation Comes and Cuts it Down while they are
in the prares

WENdesday august 15th Capt. Clark and 10 of his men and
my Self went to the Mahos Creek afishen and Caut 300 and
17 fish of Diferent Coindes ouer men has not Returnd yet

Thursday august 16th Capt Lewis and 12 of his men went
to the Creek afishen Caut 709 fish Different Coindes

Friday august 17th Continued Hear for ouer men thay did
not Return Last night Satturday augt 18th
ouer men Returnd and Brot with them the men
and Brot with them the Grand Chief of the ottoes
and 2 Loer ones and 6 youers of thare nation

[See Coues Ed. of Lewis & Clark, Vol 1, p. 79
for acent of death of Charles Floyd.]
—Feb. 5, 1894.

town and onley live about it in the winter and in the Spring
Go all of them in the praries ~~of~~ after the Buflow and dos
not Return untill the fall to meet ₐthe₍^₎ french traders thay
Rase no Corn nor aney thing ~~u~~excep Som times thuy Rase
Som Corn and then the Ottoe nation Comes and Cuts it
Down while thay are in the praries

Wendesday august 15ᵗʰ Capᵗ Clark and 10 of his men
and my Self went to the Mahas Creek a fishen and Caut
300 and 17 fish of Difernt Coindes[92] ouer men has not
Returnd yet   Thursday august 16ᵗʰ Capᵗ Lewis and
12 of his men went to the Creek a fishen Caut 709 fish
Differnt Coindes[93]

Friday august 17ᵗʰ Continued Hear for ouer men thay
did not Return Last night[94] Saturday augt 18ᵗʰ   ouer
men Returnd and Brot with them the man and Brot
with~~em~~ them ʒ the <u>Grand Chief</u> of the <u>Ottoes</u> and 2 Loer
ones and 6 youers [warriors or others] of thare nathon[95]

92. Floyd must not have been incapacitated yet—or
been struck yet—with the physical complaints
of his fatal illness if he was able to go fishing.
His reference to Clark taking ten of "his men"
rather than writing "the" or "our" men seems
odd but is consistent with the use of the possessive at that time. Another possibility is that
Lewis and Clark had unofficially divided the
party into halves regarding their command
duties and Clark had some of his men with
him, but this seems rather unlikely. Clark says
only ten men and nothing about Floyd being
with the group. In fact, the count is off if Floyd
is not one of those ten, since Clark says ten and
Floyd states ten men and himself (Clark consequently being one of those ten). The number
of fish ranges from Floyd's 317 and Clark's 318
to Whitehouse's 386 and Gass's 387. Ordway
simply writes "some 300" fish of different kinds.
Using a drag made of brush helped account for
such numbers, but it still illustrates the bounty
of the area's rivers and streams. This was Floyd's
last outing and exploring moment, unaware—as
were all the men—that his remaining days among
them were few. Clark noted on 15 August that all
the party was in good health and spirits.

93. Floyd repeats that peculiar use of the possessive
with Lewis and "his men" (other journalists do
not). If bragging rights were at stake, then Lewis
and his fishermen took the prize. All the enlisted
journalists agree that the catch was 709, but do
disagree regarding the specific number of pike
taken. Only Clark actually lists the number
of each species of fish caught, except for the
"Silver fish," but he puts the total at about 800.
Only Ordway mentions the party fiddling and
dancing on the night of the fifteenth. (Moulton,
2:485–86; 9:40; 10:28; 11:56.)

94. Actually, one of the men did return. Labiche
arrived with the message that Drouillard and
party were behind him with the Oto chiefs and
Reed. He also reported that they had appre-
hended La Liberté, but he had deceived them
and gotten away. Floyd leaves an uncharacteris-
tically large blank space at the end of this page,
as if he intended to write more but never did.
Perhaps he was already falling ill by the night of
17 August and not feeling up to writing a longer,
more descriptive entry, and when he recorded
his final entry the next day, he began a new page,
still intending to expand his entry of the day
before. (Moulton, 2:487–88.)

95. Floyd's final entry was on 18 August. He was
taken seriously ill on the morning of 19 August
and would die the next day. The other journalists provide more information on Reed's trial
and the meeting with the Oto and the Missouria
than Floyd does. It is quite possible that Floyd
was actually taking ill that evening and not up to
much more than recording the most basic of the
day's events. If so, then any celebrating he did
in honor of Lewis's birthday may have exacer-
bated his condition. Clark notes that an extra
gill of whiskey was given and there was dancing
until 11:00 p.m. Gass's biographer cites the

(continued on page 93)

Rec. of Monsier Pier Sherker 5 Carrett
of Tobacko at 3/b p. pieces $2.65
Mayie Corn & Dolie due 0,5

DeNail 2 Carrets ½ doll P. Gass. G. for T.
Dreuett Newman & Do. 50 cents Jos. Field. G. for T.
10.03 Shields & do. 50
Gibson & do 5.0
$2 n 50 Cents.

March 13th 1804

Recved of Ouen Journey
began our voyage much fetteged
after yesterday day worked

Appendix

[Inside front cover]

Rec^d of Monsier Pier Shurker 5 Carrtts
   of tobacko at 3 s/o d p^r peece

                              $ 2.55
Mayse Corn & Dolce Due   0.50

	ONail	2 Carrits	$1	dollr	P.Gass	G. for T.
Decemb	Newman	1 D°	50	Cents	Jos. Field	G. for T.
10[?]^th	Shields	1 d°	50			
1803	Gibson	1 d°	50			
			$2.50	Cents.		

———

March 13, 1804

Renued of ouer Jourey
began aur voyage much feteggdd
after yester day worke[96]

(continued from page 91)

consequences of Floyd's actions that night as bringing on his fatal illness. Gass recalled years later that Floyd, already suffering from a "delicate constitution," had been "carousing at an Indian dance" during which he became overheated and then went on guard duty during which he lay down on a sand bar. This brought on the "cramp cholic" that took his life. Could this account be true? There almost certainly is a kernel of truth in it. Gass, being in Floyd's squad and perhaps even standing guard that night, gives his recollection some validity, but such actions seem inadvisable, if not irresponsible and in violation of orders, and quite out of character for this conscientious young man. Could it be that what Gass remembered some sixty years later was Floyd succumbing to the final stage of his illness? Thus came to an abrupt end the life of Charles Floyd; and thus comes to an abrupt end the journal and adventure of this young explorer and "man of much merit." Someone other than Floyd, perhaps Draper, underlined the Oto chief. A note by Thwaites appears on the same page as Floyd's last entry referring the reader to volume one, page seventy-nine of Elliott Coues's edition of the history of the Lewis and Clark Expedition. This page contains the Biddle narrative of Floyd's death with Coues's note providing the text of the 19 and 20 August entries from Clark's fair copy journal (Codex B) regarding Floyd. (Jacob, pp. 43–44; Coues, *History of the Expedition*, 1:79.)

96. The rough notes and calculations made by Floyd on the inside cover of his journal are not entirely clear. Pier Shuker might be Pierre Chouteau, the important St. Louis businessman and Indian agent. He was an associate of Lewis and Clark and they had dealings with him while based at Camp Dubois and in St. Louis. Some of the men were apparently buying personal supplies of tobacco. Floyd calculates the cost in both the English shillings and pence and the American dollars and cents. The purchases were apparently being made during their brief stop in St. Louis on 11 December 1803 or later that month. The date appears to be 10 December, but perhaps Floyd misdated the notation by a day, therefore agreeing with their St. Louis stop, or the date is actually something other than 10 December. John Shields and George Gibson were, of course, two of Floyd's fellow "Young Kentuckians." John Newman had been recruited at Fort Massac on the lower Ohio, so he had been with the expedition since mid-November 1803. He would be courtmartialed and expelled from the Corps in October 1804 and sent back to St. Louis with the keelboat in April 1805. Hugh McNeal's unit of origin is unknown so he might have joined at either Massac or Kaskaskia

(continued on page 94)

(continued from page 93)

but would not have been one of the Tennessee recruits, since they did not arrive until later in December. Shields and Gibson would be assigned to Floyd's cousin Nathaniel H. Pryor's squad and McNeal and Newman to Floyd's. Why or how information apparently dating from December 1803 is in a journal believed to be purchased in March 1804 is not known. Perhaps Floyd recorded the accounts in the journal upon its purchase.

The notation of "P. Gass G. for T." and "Jos. Field G. for T." is believed to relate to Gass and Field being assigned guard duty in place of John Thompson, who had taken over cooking duties per orders of 8 July 1804. Those notations almost certainly do not relate to the December 1803 accounts. Perhaps the inside cover was simply convenient for Floyd to jot down the guard assignments that July or August. How the date of 13 March 1804 and the comments below it relate to Floyd's activities is a mystery. If he was up the Missouri a short way with Lewis and Clark during this time, it could relate to the mission the captains were on regarding Indian affairs. However, his statement indicating he bought the journal at Camp Dubois on that same date (from the inside back cover) prevents that possibility. Perhaps the date of purchase was not accurate or Floyd was simply writing the date and unrelated phrases on the page, possibly at different times. Parts of the phrases are ones that appear in his journal, especially his 17 June entry. There are no 13 March entries by the other journalists, so no additional information can be gained from them. A particularly intriguing clue, and perhaps sad loss to the history of the expedition, can also be seen here—the stubs of three sheets of the journal. If all three had been written on that would be an additional six journal pages. Two of the sheets definitely have writing on them, revealing only fragments of what had been written. On the reverse of the second sheet is "Shore — mile the fam of the Hassas thare we base[?]." The obverse fragment of the third sheet reads "our Dog + 2 miles I Slaied [sailed?] on the in the." The text is so brief and out of context, with no date or clue to one, that it is difficult to make much sense of these fragmentary entries or notes. The mention of Seaman is interesting. It is one of the few times he is mentioned while ascending the Missouri in 1804. (Moulton, 2:129, 179–80, 254–55, 519; Holmberg, *Dear Brother*, pp. 67, 78–79, 87–88.)

97. This page is near the back of the journal. There are eighteen blank pages between it and the page containing Floyd's last entry. Floyd obviously placed it in the back so as not to interfere with his regular entries but needing blank paper in order to figure his squad's guard duties. Why this one page from 22 June is present and not others is unknown. The weather was hot and the current strong, but nothing remarkable is recorded in any of the journals. Floyd's apparent place in the duty rotation can be fixed for at least this day or time period given his guard concerns (see the Introduction). The Field

[Page at the back of the journal]

the 22^{thd} June

Charles Floyd

Winser	$\bar{t}$	G.	22^{thd}	
R. Field	2	G.	22^{thd}	
J. Field	3		Gard for thompson	16th July
Newman	4			
Gass	5		Gard for Thompson	
mcNiel	6			
thompson	7 [97]			

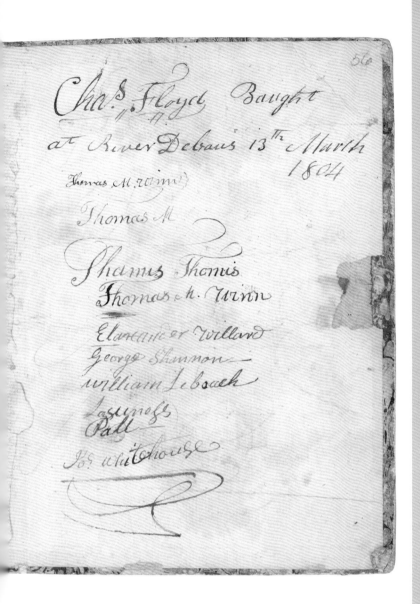

[Inside back cover]

Chaˢ Floyd Baught at River Debaus 13ᵗʰ March 1804

Thomas M. Winn

Thomas M

Thamis Thomis

Thomas M. Winn

Elaxander Willard

George Shannon

william Leboach

Lasuness

Pall —

Joˢ Whitehouse[98]

brothers, Gass, McNeal, Thompson, and Richard Windsor of his squad are listed in the 26 May detachment orders and are listed here. Missing is Francis Rivet. Per the 26 May orders, the *engagés* were included in guard duties so that would not explain his absence from Floyd's list. Perhaps he had been transferred from Floyd's squad to Pryor's or Ordway's or the *engagé* detachment by 22 June. Clark's 4 July list of the hired French boatmen lists Rivet and La Liberté as being assigned to the keelboat, so he was present on 22 June. Floyd apparently consulted this list following Thompson's assignment as cook on 8 July, since he noted Joseph Field and Gass standing guard in Thompson's place—something he also noted on the inside front cover of the journal (see preceding note). (Moulton, 2:254–56, 347.)

98. This notation and list of names are on the inside back cover of the journal. How they relate—if at all—to the notes written on the inside front cover is not known. The 13 March 1804 date appears on both and the statement saying Floyd bought what is assumed to be the journal on this date would establish its acquisition. All the names appear to be written in Floyd's hand. Thomas M. Winn was Floyd's brother-in-law. He was the postmaster for Louisville and might have been instrumental in getting young Floyd the contract as post rider between Louisville and Vincennes. Why the name is written multiple times is unknown. Why it would be written at all on a list containing expedition members is a mystery. Perhaps Winn was visiting Camp Dubois. Perhaps he had brought letters and other items from some of the explorers' friends and families at the Falls of the Ohio. He would have known Clark, possibly the Field brothers, and perhaps others in addition to his brother-in-law. Alexander H. Willard, George Shannon, William [Francois] Labiche, and Joseph Whitehouse were all members of the Corps. Jean Baptiste La Jeunesse was an *engagé*. "Pall" might be *engagé* Paul Primeau who with La Jeunesse and a few others left Fort Mandan on 6 November 1804 after being discharged from expedition service. Why the names appear in Floyd's journal is a mystery. There is no known documentary evidence that offers an explanation. The first (at least first recorded) squad assignments date from 1 April 1804 and none of the men were in Floyd's squad. The *engagés* are not listed at all in those orders. Three of the men (Willard, Whitehouse, and Labiche) were in Pryor's squad. If the seven expedition members listed (including Floyd) are counted, they form the ordered guard complement of sergeant and six privates and *engagés*; but since none of them are from Floyd's squad, that most likely is not the explanation either, unless Floyd recorded those on guard one night for some unknown reason even though he did not have the duty. The presence of Winn's name is not believed to indicate that the journal was ever in his possession. Its possible provenance is discussed in the Introduction. (Holmberg, pp. 176–77; Moulton, 2:254–55, 526, 528; 3:230–31.)

Bibliography

Ambrose, Stephen E. *Undaunted Courage: Meriwether Lewis, Thomas Jefferson, and the Opening of the American West.* New York: Simon and Schuster, 1996.

Appleman, Roy E. "Joseph and Reubin Field, Kentucky Frontiersmen of the Lewis and Clark Expedition and Their Father, Abraham." *The Filson Club History Quarterly* 49 (January 1975): 5–36.

———. *Lewis and Clark: Historic Places Associated with Their Transcontinental Exploration (1804–1806).* Washington, D.C.: U.S. Department of the Interior, National Park Service, 1975. Second printing, St. Louis, Mo.: Lewis and Clark Trail Heritage Foundation and Jefferson National Expansion Historical Association, 1993.

Betts, Robert B. *In Search of York: The Slave Who Went to the Pacific with Lewis and Clark.* Revised edition with a new epilogue by James J. Holmberg. Boulder: University Press of Colorado and Lewis and Clark Trail Heritage Foundation, 2000.

Butler, James Davie. "The New Found Journal of Charles Floyd, a Sergeant under Captains Lewis and Clark." *Proceedings of the American Antiquarian Society* 9 (April 1894): 225–52. With Appendix, 238–52.

Cartlidge, Anna Margaret, comp. "Children and Grandchildren of William and Abadiah (Davis) Floyd." Unpublished typed manuscript, 1966. Copy on file at The Filson Historical Society, Louisville, Ky.

Catlin, George. *Letters and Notes on the Manners, Customs, and Conditions of the North American Indians.* 2 vols. London: Privately published, 1841. Reprint, New York: Dover Publications, 1973.

Chittenden, Hiram M. "Erection of a Monument to Sergeant Charles Floyd," *Annual Reports of the War Department: Report of the Chief of Engineers,* Appendix JJJ. Washington, D.C.: Government Printing Office, 1901, pp. 687–88, 3827–33.

Chuinard, Eldon G. *Only One Man Died: The Medical Aspects of the Lewis and Clark Expedition.* Glendale, Calif.: Arthur H. Clark, 1979. Reprint, Fairfield, Wash.: Ye Galleon Press, 1997.

Clark, William. "Lewis and Clark Codices. Codex A—Clark. Journal, May 13, 1804–Aug. 14, 1804." Facsimile edition. Philadelphia: American Philosophical Society, 2000.

Coues, Elliott, ed. *History of the Expedition under the Command of Lewis and Clark.* 4 vols. New York: Francis P. Harper, 1893. Reprint. New York: Dover Publications, 1965, 3 vols.

———. *In Memoriam, Sergeant Charles Floyd: Report of the Floyd Memorial Association.* Sioux City, Iowa: Perkins Bros., 1897.

Draper Manuscripts, Wisconsin Historical Society, Madison (Microfilm edition at The Filson Historical Society, Louisville, Ky.), George Rogers Clark Papers, Kentucky Papers, and Draper's Historical Miscellanies collections.

Floyd Memorial Association. *In Memoriam, Sergeant Charles Floyd: Second Report of the Floyd Memorial.* Sioux City, Iowa: Perkins Bros., 1901.

Garver, Frank Harmon. "The Story of Sergeant Charles Floyd." *Proceedings of the Mississippi Valley Historical Association for the Year 1908–1909.* Vol. 2. Cedar Rapids, Iowa: Torch Press, 1910.

Harper, Josephine L. *Guide to the Draper Manuscripts.* Madison: State Historical Society of Wisconsin, 1983.

Hesseltine, William B. *Pioneer's Mission: The Story of Lyman Copeland Draper.* Madison: State Historical Society of Wisconsin, 1954.

Hinds, V. Strode. "Reconstructing Charles Floyd: Forensic Artistry Yields an Image of the Ill-fated Sergeant." With Sharon A. Long, "The Artist's Story." *We Proceeded On* 27 (February 2001): 16–19.

Holmberg, James J., " 'A Man of Much Merit': George Drouillard, the Corps of Discovery's Ace Hunter and Interpreter, Went Down Fighting in the Country He Loved." *We Proceeded On* 26 (August 2000): 8–12.

———. "Getting out the Word: New Evidence Suggests It Was Patrick Gass Who Carried William Clark's Letter Reporting on the Expedition's Return." *We Proceeded On* 27 (August 2001): 12–17.

———. "Kentucky and the Lewis & Clark Expedition." In *Lewis & Clark—Corps of Discovery, 1803–1806.* Clay City, Ky.: Back Home in Kentucky, 2003.

———. "Monument to a 'Young Man of Much Merit.'" *We Proceeded On* 22 (August 1996): 4–13.

———, ed. *Dear Brother: Letters of William Clark to Jonathan Clark.* New Haven, Conn.: Yale University Press, 2002.

Hunt, Robert R. "For Whom the Guns Sounded: Sgt. Floyd's Funeral Revisited." *We Proceeded On* 27 (February 2001): 10–15.

Jackson, Donald, ed. *Letters of the Lewis and Clark Expedition with Related Documents, 1783–1854.* Second edition. 2 vols. Urbana: University of Illinois Press, 1978.

Jacob, J. G. *The Life and Times of Patrick Gass.* Wellsburg, Va. [W. Va.]: Jacob & Smith, 1859.

Kleber, John E., ed. *The Kentucky Encyclopedia.* Lexington: University Press of Kentucky, 1992.

Lamar, Howard R., ed. *The Reader's Encyclopedia of the American West.* New York: Harper and Row, 1977.

Mordy, James C. "The Paternity of Sgt. Charles Floyd of the Lewis and Clark Expedition and the Children of Robert Clark Floyd (1752–1807) and Charles Floyd (1760–1828)." Unpublished typed manuscript, 2000. Copy on file at The Filson Historical Society, Louisville, Ky.

Moulton, Gary E. *The Lewis and Clark Journals: An American Epic of Discovery.* Lincoln: University of Nebraska Press, 2003.

———, ed. *The Journals of the Lewis and Clark Expedition.* 13 vols. Lincoln: University of Nebraska Press, 1983–2001.

The Nation 72, no. 1876 (13 June 1901): 471–72.

Osgood, Ernest Staples, ed. *The Field Notes of Captain William Clark, 1803–1805.* New Haven, Conn.: Yale University Press, 1964.

Paton, Bruce C. *Lewis & Clark: Doctors in the Wilderness.* Golden, Colo.: Fulcrum Publishing, 2001.

Peck, David G. *"Or Perish in the Attempt": Wilderness Medicine on the Lewis & Clark Expedition.* Helena, Mont.: Farcountry Press, 2002.

Ronda, James P. *Lewis and Clark among the Indians.* Lincoln: University of Nebraska Press, 1984.

Sioux City Journal (Sioux City, Iowa). 21 August 1895; 30, 31 May 1901.

Sioux City Sunday Journal (Sioux City, Iowa). 26 November 1950.

Sioux City Tribune (Sioux City, Iowa). 30 May 1901.

Skarsten, M. O. *George Drouillard, Hunter and Interpreter for Lewis and Clark and Fur Trader, 1807–1810.* Glendale, Calif.: Arthur H. Clark, 1964.

State Historical Society of Wisconsin. *Calendar of the George Rogers Clark Papers of the Draper Collection of Manuscripts.* Calendar Series, vol. 4. Madison: State Historical Society of Wisconsin, n.d. Reprint, Utica, Ky.: McDowell Publications, 1985.

———. *The Preston and Virginia Papers of the Draper Collection of Manuscripts.* Calendar Series, vol. 1. Madison: State Historical Society of Wisconsin, 1915.

Thom, James Alexander. *Sign-Talker: The Adventure of George Drouillard on the Lewis and Clark Expedition.* New York: Ballantine, 2000.

Thwaites, Reuben Gold, ed. *Early Western Travels, 1748–1846.* 32 vols. Cleveland, Ohio: Arthur H. Clark, 1904–7.

———, ed. *The Original Journals of the Lewis and Clark Expedition, 1804–1806.* 8 vols. New York: Dodd, Mead, 1904–5. Reprint, Scituate, Mass.: Digital Scanning, 2001.

Weaks, Mabel Clare. *Calendar of the Kentucky Papers of the Draper Collection of Manuscripts.* Calendar Series, vol. 2. Madison: State Historical Society of Wisconsin, 1925.

The Western Spy (Cincinnati). 26 June; 3 July 1805.

Yater, George H. "Nine Young Men from Kentucky." In George H. Yater and Carolyn S. Denton, *Nine Young Men from Kentucky,* supplement to *We Proceeded On,* WPO Publication no. 11. Great Falls, Mont.: Lewis and Clark Trail Heritage Foundation, 1992.

Index

Discove...

Exploration

The Corps of Discovery traveled up the Missouri River, over the Rocky Mountains, and down the Snake and Columbia Rivers. Despite great physical challenges, isolation, and near starvation at times, the expedition mapped vast territories of the West. In November 1805, they reached their ultimate destination, the Pacific Ocean. The words of their journals provide exciting glimpses of their remarkable adventures.

Indian Country

The Corps of Discovery encountered the diversity and generosity of many Indian Nations as they traveled across the land and waters. The expedition survived and succeeded because of the shelter, supplies, good will, and cooperation of Native American people they met. Now, as then, the people, cultures, and land have much to share.

Homecoming

With the Missouri River's current, the Corps of Discovery covered up to 70 miles a day and returned to St. Louis on September 23, 1806. The expedition had covered nearly 5,000 miles of territory in over 2 years. Their detailed journals contributed important information about the land, its geographic features, its natural resources, and its native peoples.

Preparation

Recruitment

Exploration and
Homecoming

Indian Reservation

Louisiana Purchase
Boundary

Lewis and Clark
National Historic Trail